THE WEALTHY PEASANT

BY

SHAUNA MADSEN

The Wealthy Peasant

Madsen, Shauna

ISBN 978-0-9937146-1-0 (paperback)
ISBN 978-0-9937146-3-4 (hardcover)
ISBN 978-0-9937146-0-3 (ebook)
ISBN 978-0-9937146-2-7 (audiobook)

Edited by Publish and Promote
Cover design by Publish and Promote
Interior layout and design by Davor Nikolic

Printed and bound in Canada

Note to the reader: The events in this book are based on the author's memories from her perspective. Certain names have been changed to protect the identities of those mentioned. Any similarity to real persons, places, incidents, or actions is coincidental. The information is provided for educational and inspirational purposes only.

I dedicate this book to my mentor, teacher, best friend, number one fan, and cheerleader my mother, Rosemary Martha.

I'm grateful I chose you!

.

TABLE OF CONTENTS

INTRODUCTION

Everyone has a story, but who spends most of their lives dissecting, reflecting, and observing current circumstances or past events? Not many, and you know why? It's painful shit. Whether we ponder the relationships we are in now or the ones we blew up in the middle of the living room floor on the way to the taxi patiently running up the meter out front, what do we look for so we don't make the same mistake again? Where do we even begin?

How many times have you said to yourself, "If only I knew then what I know now!"?

Hindsight is a lousy teacher. Teachers are there to show you the way, like a mentor or a coach. They aren't there to press your nose to the rearview mirror, reminding you of the loss, grief, and torment you either caused or received. Teachers pre-pave your way with ideas, lessons, and knowledge to help move you forwards. They don't expect you to get it all right 100% of the time. Still, if you get it wrong 99% of the time, they will give you a failing mark. Maybe not these days, since kids aren't allowed to fail or get a zero on a test, but I tell you, the teachers I had in school weren't scared to fail me, call me a failure, or hand out the strap when they thought I deserved it.

Everyone has a story, and I don't know a soul who has had a storybook childhood, except my grandchildren. If I could come back as anything next time around, I would be one of my daughter's children. Her kids have parents who listen, interpret, spend time understanding and communicating, and they laugh, play, and allow their kids to be themselves and grow into confident little people.

OH, if I knew then what I know now. I would likely have written a trilogy by now.

I was afraid to tell my story, and I've buried it for so long. I've transferred it from handwritten loose-leaf, between two PCs, across four external backup drives, onto my first Mac in 2012, my second in 2016, my third in 2019, and finally to my MacBook Pro in 2020. I avoided my book until it dawned on me that I'd been creating distractions out of fear—fear disguised as distractions because I was afraid of being found out.

You see, I've held some impressive jobs. I've been an entrepreneur for more than thirty years, and I've spoken on stage at business conferences with hundreds of businesswomen listening to me share tips on building their business. I've won awards, I've been interviewed on TV and radio, and I live in a lovely home on an acreage. People see me as successful and wealthy by their definition.

My fear was cemented in the idea that people would judge me for being married multiple times. Four marriages constitute multiple times, right? I was afraid clients, after spending thousands of dollars with me to teach them how to build a business, would reject me when I leaked the sombre truth of my Grade 9 education. I was fearful of what my family might say when I opened the door to our past and let the world peek inside.

It took cancer, a heart attack, a pandemic, and a team of angels on my shoulders whispering in both ears, or more like screaming, "YOUR REARVIEW MIRROR IS A GIFT. SHARE IT!" to finally write my story.

So, I responded, "Fine, fine, I'm doing it," and I took a trip to Costa Rica for a writer's retreat to reignite my story. If it can help you take steps toward a life you love, I've done my job, and I will kindly give the angels a much-deserved holiday.

I want to share how a slight shift in how we see ourselves can change the course of everything. A dysfunctional childhood does not define who we are. Abusive relationships are not an excuse to remain a victim. A lack of education is not a reason to settle for mediocrity or accept less than what we dream for our future.

I didn't write *The Wealthy Peasant* to say, "I did it, so you can too," although I believe that to be true with all my heart. I wrote my story because the world is a mess, and I know the ripple effect we make by becoming the best versions of ourselves. It is my earnest hope that enough people become their best selves so the world pays attention and wants a little piece of what we have, through attraction rather than promotion.

Why *The Wealthy Peasant?*

Society defines wealth as an abundance of valuable possessions or money, and a peasant is a term often used to describe a poor person of low social standing.

The status quo dictates that we measure success by material gain, and society passes judgment based on outward appearances. Whether it's the car we drive, the clothes we wear, the colour of our skin, our spiritual beliefs, or the number of followers we have on social media—we are judged. I have been persecuted for defending my values, exiled for believing in God the "wrong way," ridiculed for being myself, and beaten for speaking my truth. Oh, and humiliated for having 425,000 km on my Jetta. WTF?

True wealth is not found on the bottom line of a spreadsheet. It is internal. It is a flint that sparks our genius and illuminates our path. It is an attitude that carries us, fuels our persistence, and feeds our tenacity. Wealth is an attitude and a knowing. We can share it and never lose it. It grows with every step we take. Nobody can take it from us.

I learned the hard way, in every way.

As a child, I escaped reality with the help of *Nancy Drew* and my collection of fairy tales. I internalized the romantic endings of each book, adopting the idea that good always prevails over evil. I imagined myself as the good witch or the princess whose dreams came true if she believed in the possibility of a happily ever after.

My mom said I followed the rules of the relationship formula by marrying representations of my father. And I didn't do it once; I did it repeatedly, thinking each time would be different. I clung to my childhood ideas that good will always prevail over evil, and all I had to do was believe. If I focused on the good, and I became whatever I thought was the person I was supposed to be inside the relationship, we would live happily ever after.

I didn't see my father's habits and qualities in the men I was attracted to until the end of each relationship. I was unknowingly attracted to the familiar, and the true qualities of each man remained hidden below the surface at the beginning of each relationship. I may have wanted the fairy tale, but I was drawn to what I had grown up with, and my dad set the stage.

He was an abusive alcoholic, absent as a father, and controlling as a husband. He quit drinking when I was fourteen, but that was too late for me and my three siblings. The damage was done, and it took each of us years to repair some of that damage. My mom was a child herself when she married my dad at the age of seventeen, and her father was an alcoholic, so she only knew what she had grown up with.

We didn't know what we didn't know, and so we believed our lives were the norm. If someone had asked me if I was happy as a child, I wouldn't have understood the question. What was happy? Was it a feeling, like the pain of loneliness that gnawed at my insides?

My parents broke the cycle of alcoholism that plagued both their families for generations. When Dad quit drinking, our family fell apart, Mom and Dad divorced, and we all began our own journeys to recovery. It all had to happen exactly the way it did. My dad has grown into a wonderful man and has helped hundreds, if not thousands of alcoholics live a life of sobriety. The rest of us, including my beautiful mother, have put in the work, made the effort to become better versions of ourselves, and we have reaped many rewards.

My mom once told me the world wasn't ready for my story. But now, with all that is happening in the world, my story doesn't seem so horrific. People have become desensitized to horrors of all descriptions, so the time has come for *The Wealthy Peasant*. My story seems like a preamble with everything from emotional and physical abuse, single parenting, choosing between adoption and abortion, spirituality, religion, rape, survival, workplace harassment, poverty, homelessness, alcoholism, marriage, more marriage, abandonment, failure, success, fear, love, and heartache. My story or parts of it will likely be familiar to you, and I hope I can give you a seed of inspiration if you are stuck and unsure how to navigate the next steps forward.

Disclaimer #1:

Spirituality and religion are two very different concepts to me. Whether you belong to a church or not, believe in fate, destiny, God, a higher power, a Great Spirit, or you believe in nothing, or something completely different, it doesn't matter. I talk about my own spirituality, partially because I think it's a fascinating topic but also as the thread that ties my stories together to make sense of it all.

I have very broad beliefs about most things in life because I've spent more than fifty years dissecting, reflecting, observing, and consciously making choices to sort through the pile of shit between my ears. I've discovered profound truths about life, love, and relationships that many people can't see, take for granted, or can't be bothered to explore. This life we live is multidimensional and ever-expanding, and the wealth you hold inside of you is all you need to be, do, and have everything you can imagine. It doesn't matter what your past is telling you, and the things you worry about for the future do nothing more than waste your precious time and energy.

Disclaimer #2:

My stepfather used to say that if I didn't have chaos in my life, I'd create it. That was true to a degree, but in my defence, I was diagnosed with ADHD (attention deficit hyperactivity disorder) at the ripe age of fifty-five. Over the years, I've learned coping skills to work with the squirrel I call Surel, who has been freeloading for years, stealing ideas, creating distractions, and causing all kinds of havoc for me. This is a disclaimer to give you a heads-up on how I write, tell stories, and pretty much live my life. I don't apologize for it, except when I miss an appointment or forget to put the milk back in the fridge. To keep a positive spin on what others see as a "disorder," I have relabelled ADHD as *Awesome Divas Have Dreams*, and I am sticking with that.

Disclaimer #3:

A few names have been changed because it was a smart thing to do.

MAYBE I'M AN ALIEN

I would take my pillow and blanket, along with my dog, Duke, out into the backyard. On a warm summer night, this was my favourite place to be, alone under the stars with my best friend. I loved setting up a bed on the lounge chair parallel to the patio with distance enough that the big sky was unimpeded by the roofline. Each time, I challenged myself to see how long I would hold out and see if I could make it to morning before heading into the security of my bed, and not because I was scared. I like the dark. But there were times I found myself in strange places instead of in my bed.

As I set up my open-air room, settling Duke on the lounge chair at my feet with strategic balance so not to tip either of us off and onto the cool grass, I thought about my experience at my friend's house a couple of weekends prior. Her mom found me sleepwalking in their backyard at three in the morning, my pillow under my arm and head tilted toward the sky. I awoke when she came running and grabbed my arm, shocking me awake with her motherly tone.

"What are you doing? Are you crazy?"

I had no idea what was going on or why I was outside in the middle of the night. She placed her hand gently between my shoulder blades, guiding me back to the house.

She whispered, "You're a strange child."

I was relieved my friend didn't tell the kids at school. But her mom made it clear I wasn't welcome back until I was finished with my "episodes" as she called them.

The sky was a white blanket of stars, with wisps of white translucent clouds. I pulled the fleece blanket up to my chin, and a familiar sensation drained tension and my friend's backyard from my mind. I now felt present and attuned to my surroundings, with the silhouette of poplars, almost motionless, framing the backyard on three sides. Panning the night sky revealed a one-dimensional layer of dots in various sizes. The panoramic view seemed to shift, exposing more stars, with a few shining brighter and more prominent than the minuscule, fuzzy, dim dots. I realized there were, in fact, layers, not a single flat sheet of stars as I had initially thought.

I closed one eye and raised my hand high, drawing a line with my index finger. I joined the stars to complete what I decided to be my very own constellation. My mind paused with a thought: *If there is a distance between them*, I questioned, *what is behind the stars I see?* I continued asking: *If there is more of the same behind those, what is behind those? Where does it all end? How can it end, because if it did, what would be on the other side? Nothing? What is nothing? Nothing must be something.*

I travelled in my mind to what infinity might look like, the possibility that there is no end to the universe. In awe, I gazed up into the white mass for what seemed like forever when something appeared. Three white stars converged together into a triangle, far above the earth, directly above me. They danced together for a few seconds and, in a flash, darted in three different directions, disappearing in a blur.

I lay there for a few minutes, absorbing what had just happened. I mulled this over in my mind. *Is this real?* I argued with my flash of doubt. *Of course, it's real. I saw it. I'm wide awake. Stars don't do that; Planes don't do that.* I looked down at Duke curled up at my feet, and he hadn't moved a muscle.

Nonchalantly, I said to my loyal friend, "Well, I guess we aren't alone."

That night sparked three weeks of restless nights and a series of dreams and nightmares I am sure Stephen King would revel in. It was all very real to me, and I'm sure I was awake to experience floating heads above my parents' bed when I ran into the room, scared out of my wits.

I was twelve years old; What did I know about the four stages of sleep my parents talked about? Nothing.

All I knew, with the most profound conviction, was that this shit was happening.

Sleeping with the light on didn't scare away the faceless, motionless figure that laid beside me almost every night. Breaking free of my terror with my eyes glued shut, I reached beside me and felt it. Someone or something was lying there. My little sister became accustomed to sleeping in the bright room, as the light was on every night. She occupied the lower bunk, and I draped a blanket from my bed to block the brightness for her. Through my terrors, she didn't move. She was completely unaware of what I was experiencing. Maybe I was dying.

With my eyes closed, the more I tried to focus my attention on anything but the moment, heavy grey blanketed figures rushed toward my face. I forced my eyes open to the brightly lit room and jumped from my bunk to the floor, swung my door wide open, and ran into my parents' bedroom, again greeted by floating heads above their bed, and there was one familiar face: Mrs. Wahn, my French teacher. Mom and Dad just lay there, sleeping, completely unaware of what was happening above them.

Mom and Dad woke to my whispering, "Mom, Dad, it's happening again."

I was shaking like a leaf while the three of us sat at the dining room table. Dad passed me a cigarette.

"I know you are smoking behind our backs, so you might as well smoke in front of us. Maybe it will calm your nerves. Besides, if you smoke in front of us, it's less likely you'll burn the house down."

I relaxed back into the chair, inhaling the familiar hot taste of Mom's homemade menthol cigarettes. I knew them well. My brother Blaine and I stole one or two at a time, and often.

On occasion, when Mom drove to town to run errands, we would pull her cigarette machine out from under the kitchen sink and roll a few, tucking them into our hiding spot in the shed.

Mom and Dad discussed the week of my terrors, wondering out loud, "Should we or shouldn't we take her to a shrink?"

I relaxed further into my seat, crossing my legs and tucking my feet up under my thighs as I drew long hauls of menthol deep into my lungs—with permission.

The following night, Mom made me a bed on the couch while Blaine watched TV in Dad's La-Z-Boy, and it didn't take long for me to fall asleep. I floated up, higher and higher off the couch. Visions of stars filled my mind's eye and brought me back to my night outside with Duke under the stars.

The stars seemed so close I could touch them, and as I reached out—BANG! My physical body lept from the couch like a fish, and I landed on the floor. The stars weren't stars at all; They were the tiny sparkly particles in the stippled ceiling. I awoke to my brother screaming for Mom, horrified at what had just happened. He avoided me for a few days, thinking I was possessed. I told him aliens visited me, and he told me I was weird. Since Dad gave me a cigarette the night floating heads filled the room, and they felt they needed to be fair, Blaine had permission to smoke cigarettes in front of Mom and Dad too. This was a significant win for the two of us, and our older brother couldn't blackmail us any longer when he caught us smoking behind the garage.

THE TREE
AND ITS ACORNS

A binging alcoholic father made him a horrible dad and an even worse husband. He spent weeks away from home, either working as a boilermaker in some remote gas plant, binging with his friends, or both, leaving Mom to contend with my two older brothers, Jimmy and Blaine, my younger sister, Kimberley, and me. I wasn't just a middle child—I was in the middle of everything. One time, I stood between a machete-wielding brother chasing the eldest through the house. Jimmy tormented Blaine continuously, and this fight was Blaine getting revenge. Instead, Jimmy attempted to escape and fell against the wall at the end of the hall, cracking the paint from ceiling to floor. We called it a machete; It wasn't a machete but the two-foot knife Mom used to cut pizza.

Jimmy was more privileged than Blaine and me, as we were the middle kids. He was lucky to participate in the sport he wanted, like hockey, whereas Blaine endured tap dancing classes with me. Neither of us wanted to be there and quit before we could be humiliated in public at the year-end performance. Four years behind me, Kimberley spent much of her time either with her imaginary companion or at sleepovers with her friends.

Practicing his hockey slap shots on the lawn, Jimmy coerced me into stopping the shots as his goalie, and his mighty slapshots were painful.

When Mom went to town, I was left at home with my brothers, who entertained themselves by tossing me in the dryer or dragging me behind the tractor in a sleeping bag. I was too ashamed to bring my friends to our place, in fear of my dad coming home in a drunken stupor or worse, a dry drunk rage when he either showered us with gifts he couldn't afford out of guilt, or he would belittle me in front of the adults in the room by saying things like, "How dare you even think of crying, you baby. If you want something to cry about, I'll give it to you."

Dad quit drinking when I was between the ages of fourteen and fifteen, cleaning up his act in time to agree to pull me from school at the principal's request. I was sitting in Grade 10 math class, staring at the algebra questions on the test in front of me. They looked like hieroglyphics since I hadn't attended any classes in the first three months of the school year. I rested my chin on the desk, and I made the decision, telling myself, *That's it, I have to get my act together*.

At that moment, the intercom came bellowing in the classroom, "Shauna Madsen—office, please."

As I walked to the office, a list of possibilities came to mind. I could get another detention: Had I reached the point of no return? Or maybe they were considering me for a no-show award: Did they even notice me missing? Maybe someone saw our group walking uptown for fries and gravy. Upon further thought, I settled on the most likely reason for another trip to the office: another strap from our librarian, Mr. Fredrick.

He was the strap sergeant who relished on waiting for the next victim to come into the library. He would escort me to his office, wearing his five-day-a-week forest green polyester suit.

He'd instruct me to sit in the wooden chair against the wall; A small stool made of solid wood sat beside it. Silent and in slow motion, for effect I'm sure, he'd pull the well-worn, pliable two-inch leather strap from his desk. He worked hard to portray himself as a strong authoritarian, puffing his chest, looking down his slender nose; *Has he ever cracked a smile?* I wondered. *If I had to work at this library,* I thought, *I'd want to hand out the straps too.* I concluded that he was likely bored out of his mind, sitting behind his desk, surrounded by books he wouldn't ever read and sorting and shelving the ones he retrieved from the return bin. Other than handing out the strap, what else would give him any job satisfaction?

"Do you know why you are here?" he always asked.

A stupid rhetorical question: I was there because he loved handing out the strap every chance he had, but I wouldn't say it. I'd either shake my head to see if *he* knew why I was there, or nod, acknowledging he saw that I goofed off in his library.

As he did every other time before, he stepped up on the little wooden stool with firmly planted feet and told me to hold out my right hand. Since this was a regular occurrence, as an accomplished recipient, I knew what to expect and what the best response should be. His delivery method was a running joke among my friends, and we mimicked his technique on the school grounds. I learned to hold my palm as flat and tight as possible, like feeding popcorn to a camel. Poised and ready, he'd stand tall, swing his strap back like he was about to fire a fastball, and jump from his stool, connecting the leather to my outstretched hand with a loud SNAP!

I'd react with a scream, for his benefit alone. I learned that if he saw that it didn't hurt, he'd do it again and again. So, I would play it up with a whole lot of whaling. (If he were either of our math or science teachers, he would have known how much force he lost using the stool, the jump, and the arm swings.) We would then move to the next hand and finish the ritual, and I'd be free to go.

The last time I received the gift of leather across my palms, it was for clowning around in drama class. In art class, we had to colour between the lines, so it makes sense that our drama class wasn't a place to act out either.

I don't recall all the reasons for my many punishments in the library, but the experience added value to my survival kit. I wore two-sided armour; The outer layer kept me safe and protected, while my inner layer was sewn together with insecurity, doubt, and loneliness, all of which were seeping through and possessing me to act out as a class clown or a rebellious smart-ass.

Dad was sitting at the desk facing the principal when I walked in. I stood waiting for a pause in their conversation.

The principal shot me a sideways glance as he said to my dad, "She is wasting our time. We suggest you agree to take her out."

The principal passed a paper across his desk for my dad to sign. I was too young to be officially kicked out, so by law, my dad had to make the formal request. I was an involuntary drop-out. Only twenty minutes ago, I was promising myself I was going to get it together. Too late. I'm sure the principal was happy to see me go. He caught me with my friends either skipping school or smoking pot under the stairs in the west wing or forging the odd parent's signature.

Dad walked me to my locker, and I cleaned my belongings out and tossed the half-eaten sandwich and smelly lunch bags in the hallway trash can. I figured I would either get a lecture or the silent treatment when we left the front of the school and walked to his truck.

Instead, my dad put his hand on my shoulder and said, "You're not cut out for school, just like I wasn't. Look at me, I only have Grade 8, and I turned out just fine."

Way to parent, Dad. What I wanted from my dad was to fight for me. To push me, tell me I had what it takes to do whatever I wanted. I wanted him to support the opinion of my favourite teacher, Mrs. Hatridge; I was creative with so much potential, that's what she said, and that's what she wrote on my report card. I wanted him to care enough to ask me what I wanted. I wanted him to be my dad.

He did the best with the hand he was dealt, with the habits and addictions his parents passed along to him. Dad came from a long line of heavy drinkers, plus he was a product of his environment. Grandpa was a farmer and fond of moonshine, which he conjured up in the shed behind the house. One sunny afternoon, Dad played on the beach that bordered their property, 200 metres from the moonshine shed where Grandpa spent hours cooking and perfecting his brew. On this day, as Dad drew circles in the sand with his favourite stick, Grandpa walked back and forth from the house to the moonshine shed.

Grandpa's concoction was interrupted by the police car rolling up to the back of the house. The officer stepped out onto the driveway. Grandpa slinked from the shed, quickly closing the door behind him. He walked briskly toward the officer, politely greeted him, and held him in conversation at the hood of the police cruiser. The officer was looking for someone in the area. Dad was still squatting in the sand, half-heartily spinning his stick while his focus was on the two men exchanging words, nods, and hand gestures. Reading his father's body language, Dad sensed Grandpa had positioned himself to keep the officer's attention and sightline away from the moonshine shed. The curious white smoke curling from the pipe on the roof was getting thicker and thicker by the moment.

The officer thanked Grandpa, returned to his car, and proceeded up the driveway. He watched as the officer turned onto the main road and diminish to a speck toward town. Moments later, Grandpa turned to the shed in time to see the roof explode, spewing shingles and wood splinters far into the sky. The front door collapsed on the ground.

That was the day my dad took his first drink, scooping a cup of moonshine from the broken still while his father cleared the yard from the aftermath of the explosion.

Dad told me this moment was the trigger that changed his life. That first drink sparked the rush, and the adrenalin coursed through Dad's six-year-old scant body, imprinting a desire for more and creating a lifelong cycle of self-destructive choices and alcoholic episodes. Dad explained, as he learned from AA, it was common for alcoholics to stunt their intellectual growth, holding them at the level they were when they started drinking; It would remain there until they committed to recovery and a program like Alcoholics Anonymous, where they find their higher power.

We didn't live in a faith-based home, and Dad made a point of criticizing any form of religion or spiritual teaching. I don't know why I believed in God at such a young age when no one else did in the family. Maybe it was my extra-terrestrial experience, and the aliens dropped something from the sky, invading my body with this connection I had to something greater than myself, whom I chose to call God. My brothers caught me praying one night at bedtime, and they teased me relentlessly for weeks, so I talked to God in private, on walks with Duke, and I remember asking God why I felt so sad all the time. I often wondered whether other kids were as lonely as me.

With Dad in the AA program, he went to meetings daily, if not twice a day. He shared his remorse, and at times, he overshared stories with his daughter who didn't need to hear them, yet I loved to talk about his spiritual journey since I was the only one in the house that had any spiritual connection growing up.

Whenever the topic of God or spirituality came into conversations, my ears perked up like satellite dishes spinning to catch a signal for clarity. I didn't know if I believed in the same God as the people who went to church. I did know I had a relationship with something or someone that I could feel. Even though I thought it, I was searching for a more defined explanation of who it was that I called God.

Dad shared what he learned, and I came to believe what Dad told me. His new code and mantra was, "It's God's will." This applied to everything and anything. Things that had happened or were about to, or things that didn't happen the way you wanted—all of it was God's will. His belief system, which was passed down to me, had the potential for the same outcome as giving a five-year-old the keys to a Maserati. It's one thing to have faith, but it's quite another to hand over all responsibility to unseen forces, and I didn't have to be accountable since everything was God's will.

I embraced Dad's code for many years. When things went well, it was God's will, and when life went sideways, that too was God's will. When everything blew up out of control, it was God's will, and whatever happened next, that too, if it was meant to be, was God's will. Good God!

TAKING FLIGHT

When I was twelve years old, I wanted God to take me away, and when I found a bottle of Tylenol, I figured if I took enough, I wouldn't wake up. That was the plan.

I was an empty, lonely little girl and had no one to talk to or confide in. Even if I'd had someone, what would I have said? I couldn't talk to my parents; I didn't know how. Besides, my dad didn't allow us to express our feelings, and tears at the table triggered, "Go to your room if you're going to cry. I can give you something to cry about."

I grabbed the bottle, a glass of water, and a blanket, and I went to the front yard, where I spread things out on a patch of soft grass under the blazing afternoon sun. After popping a handful of Tylenol in my mouth and washing it down with water, I laid on the blanket, staring directly into the sun, and I gave God permission to take me away; I was ready. Two hours passed, and then I woke up with a terrible sunburn, all alone, and pissed off at God.

My next plan involved moving out. I was thirteen years old, not sure where I would go or how to get there, but I decided that killing myself wasn't working, so I must have a purpose, or God would have released me from my bondage. I wasn't sure how to pull it off, but I would design furniture, live in New York in an apartment with brick walls, and become famous. I loved the modern style of furniture they had on the starship Enterprise in my favourite program, *Star Trek*. I felt at home watching that program. After my experience with what I came to believe was a celestial encounter, I was all over anything science fiction.

The floating head of my French teacher that I saw when I was twelve never visited again, and I squeaked through French with a below-average grade. I wouldn't say I liked school, but what I loved was my English class with Mrs. Hatridge, who took me under her wing and saw something special that no one else took the time to recognize.

She knew how I loved creating art projects and writing stories and essays. She understood me. In contrast, my brothers deconstructed or destroyed any of the art they found lying around or cut my Barbies' hair off and drew all over their bodies with a permanent black marker.

Mrs. Hatridge invited me to stay behind after class to help, engaging me to come up with ideas for her events, creating announcements, posters, and decorations. On days I stayed after school, she offered to drive me home, and without us ever talking about it, I knew she had a pretty good idea of what home life was like for me. The signs and signals were evident to her since her former husband was a raging alcoholic. I worked hard for her and wanted to please her and make her proud; I loved the attention she paid me. Approval and acceptance were all I wanted, and she gave them freely.

My mom may not have been a saint; However, she does deserve a medal of honour for valour, dedication, perseverance, patience, and any other adjective to describe an incredible woman, mother, and wife. She was and is talented, creative, and very resourceful. She made my clothes for years as a young girl. I wore my brothers' hand-me-down pants and the creations from Mom's busy sewing machine—nothing like the clothing other girls were wearing. For my Grade 9 graduation celebration, she found a pattern and made a white eyelet dress with bright orange ruffles wrapped diagonally across my body from my waist to my shoulder. Since I was starting puberty, I was built like a box and carried enough extra weight that the two bullies in my social studies class called me Porky. This dress my mom created with love, I think, made me look like a giant Creamsicle as I walked across the stage to accept my certificate. There was laughter. I blew it off by doing a little jig on stage, even though my inside voice was telling me to get the hell out of there. All the other girls in the school were wearing beautiful gowns and pumps, which were the latest in fashion for women's shoes—delicate tapered one-inch heels. Mine were sandals with one-inch square wooden heels that sounded like horses' hooves on the lacquered stage floor.

Living in rural Alberta, in a hamlet called Ircton, our yard was less than an acre but enough to keep Mom busy. She immersed herself in gardening, cooking, and sewing. Looking back, these were her solo interests to maintain some degree of happiness in a loveless marriage. She grew rows of peas, carrots, lettuce, and potatoes, and I recall Swiss chard in the mix too. I hated working in the garden and didn't like weeding or hilling potatoes. I enjoyed picking peas for dinner though, eating more than I brought to the house.

Mom tried year after year to grow strawberries, and year after year, Dad would come along with the rototiller and grumble them under. He said he didn't see them. Mom's efforts went unnoticed by us kids because we didn't know any better, but Dad didn't have an excuse; He always got his way, and his own needs trumped everyone else's. Mom still lived at home when she met Dad and went straight into marriage at seventeen years old, living in Dad's shadow for twenty-five years, doing all the work at home and raising four challenging kids. She endured Dad's put-downs, "I earn the money around here," a familiar rant to justify buying himself expensive guitars and denying Mom any extras.

⁂

I may have been predisposed to have a deep love for animals, passed down through the genes, for which I can thank my dad. His love of animals began with his first love, Alan, the bull.

When Dad was eight, he and Grandpa visited their neighbouring farmer to watch the birthing of a calf. They rushed to the door of the barn, gently pushing it open to see the farmer behind the cow with his arm buried deep to his shoulder, massaging and pulling on the calf whose legs were dangling from his mother; It was a breach. The whaling sound from the mother in labour echoed from the barn and across the yard.

Grandpa jumped in to help, and he pulled on the calf's legs; After several forceful tugs, the little body slipped out and onto the straw floor.

"Well, this one is too small. We won't be keeping this calf," the farmer grumbled in frustration after the long and painful labour. "She may not be able to carry another after a labour like that."

Dad piped up and asked, "Why won't you keep him?"

"He's a runt and a male, and the two don't go together. We will fatten him up enough for dinner."

My dad didn't fully understand what the farmer meant, and so he asked on their walk home. Grandpa explained that when a calf is a male and a runt, he won't grow into a bull of any use and will cost the farmer money instead of making the farmer money. They will butcher him as a calf and either keep the meat or sell it.

"NO, that can't happen. Can I have the calf, please?" Dad begged my grandpa. "I will look after him. He doesn't need to be a large bull. He can be a small bull; That would be better anyway," he said, nodding to the path in front of them, kicking the odd rock. "Please?" he pleaded.

Grandpa didn't reply. He hadn't yet talked to my dad about his plans to move out West with his older sons and leave my dad behind with Uncle Ben. Alberta was booming, jobs were available for any type of labour, and the oil companies were hiring thousands of men.

Two weeks passed when Grandpa walked through the front gate with the calf in tow. Dad jumped to his feet, dropping the stick he used to carve circles in the red earth on his solo playdates.

Grandpa smiled. "He is yours; I paid one dollar for him."

Dad took the rope from Grandpa, thanking him over and over, and grinning from ear to ear as he stared into the calf's big brown eyes.

Scratching him behind the ear, he told his new pet, "Your name is Alan."

Dad's love for Alan the bull deepened as he grew into a full-grown bull, small in farmer measure and large in pet stature. For eight years, they were inseparable. He followed Dad everywhere, greeting him at the gate when he came home from school and walking him to the end of the lane every morning.

Living with Uncle Ben was good, but Dad missed his brothers, and at the age of sixteen, he followed Grandpa and his brothers out west, leaving Alan the bull with Uncle Ben.

Dad was one of four Madsen boys and grew up on Prince Edward Island, off the East Coast of Canada. Grandpa was an immigrant from Denmark settling on Prince Edward Island. There he met Nanny, who loved to drink, and when she did, she was mean. I never liked her, yet I felt a little guilt for my lack of empathy when she died one night while I had one of my sleepouts in the backyard with Duke under the stars.

The phone in the house rang around 3:00 a.m. A wave rushed through me, and I knew at that moment that Nanny had died unexpectedly. How I knew, I didn't know, but I knew. My mom came to the door and suggested I come into the house for the night. She sat me down to give me the news. Before she could say anything, I told her that I knew Nanny had died.

She asked me, "How do you know?"

"I just know. I felt it."

We had little over one acre to work with, but Dad maximized the space to accommodate a variety of animals, including Barney the horse, bought from the slaughterhouse for $25. We quickly learned why he was in the slaughterhouse: He was an asshole horse. When Jimmy took him out for what should have been a leisurely ride, he'd bolt toward the trees to brush him off under the branches, and then he'd run away. He'd then stop in the field to graze on thistle lining the barbed wire fenceline, and he'd taunt Dad and Jimmy as they got close enough to grab the reins, then bolt again.

Dad built a pen for Wilbur the pig. I was in love with that pig, and his pen was the first place I went every day after school—until one day, I went to the pen and Wilbur was gone. Dad announced over breakfast one morning that the bacon on our plate used to live in the pen. I was heartbroken and began to cry. Dad sent me to my room as there was no crying at the table.

I'm not sure how the wild birds in our area would have survived without my brothers' help; They were forever bringing home young pigeons, claiming they fell from their nest. When they raided the crow's nest, it was payday for everyone. They brought home a young crow, still in pinfeathers, named him Herbie Miller, and we fed him baby pablum with a small spoon until he was strong enough to eat real crow food. He lived in the chicken coop with the bantam chickens, picking up their language as crows do. He mimicked the chickens, the rooster, and the squeaky screen door. He followed us around like a dog with wings. Herbie loved Dad, and I was happy about that and pretty sure he wouldn't end up on our breakfast plate one morning—who eats crow? Herbie could sense from a mile away when Dad was coming home and would fly to meet him, landing on the driver's side mirror for the ride home. I had to admit, he was more interesting than Wilbur. He had far more personality than the two rabbits my parents agreed to if I built the rabbit pen myself, which I did. Dad cut the outhouse in half, saving the top as a doghouse that none of the dogs would use, so I padded the doghouse with straw, constructed chicken wire walls for their outdoor patio with an opening for a door, and the rabbits were mine.

Herbie foraged for shiny objects in Dad's shop when the door was left open and waited for Mom to finish hanging clothes on the line before flying over to pull the pins off, and with a squawk, he tilted his head curiously or mischievously to watch each piece of clothing fall to the ground. Even as a full-grown crow, Mom invited him into the house and filled a large basin with warm water on the dining room table for his bath; He soaked everything within ten feet.

Dad spent hours building a heated birdhouse, and Herbie helped, jumping on Dad's head and flying in and out of the house, getting in the way. When it was finally finished, Herbie wanted nothing to do with it and retreated to the chicken coop. When Herbie disappeared, Mom assured me that he wouldn't show up on our dinner table like Wilbur, and he must have found a girlfriend and flew away. He was so tame, he may have snuck up behind a coyote to make a friend, ending his life at the coyote's dinner table. I'll never know.

Mom softened the blow each time we lost a pet. She enjoyed Herbie, but she loved her cocker spaniel, Misty, who sat at her feet after dinner to share butterscotch lifesavers while we watched TV. We had a beautiful collie, Josephine, with a bad habit of chasing vehicles, including the grain trucks that travelled back and forth in front of our house daily, heading to the grain elevators a half-mile down the road. She was pregnant when she was hit by a truck and killed, and poor Mom cleaned up the remains before we got off the bus from school that day. We saw her with the wheelbarrow, a blanket covering all that she'd scooped up, and she was sobbing. With the loss of Josephine and then after Misty died, Mom never got close to another animal in the same way.

As I moved up two grades to Grade 9 and then my milestone year in Grade 10 when Dad pulled me from school, I immersed myself in a hard life with a new group of friends—the ones you don't want to bring home to meet your mom. All the while, and unbeknownst to us kids, Mom and Dad were splitting up. Suddenly, my sister and I were going to be moving to the big city. My brothers would stay behind on the acreage with Dad. What the hell?!

My mom's world flipped upside down. Since Dad never allowed her control over money, she was forced to learn the very basics of everything. Renting a place as a single mother at the time was difficult, and the landlords would ask Mom stupid questions like, "Who will mow the lawn?" Clearly, they had no idea what my mother was capable of and whom they were dealing with.

From the outside, Mom looked ok; She seemed healthy, she had it together, she had a job, and eventually found a townhouse for us to rent in the city's northside. I'm sure it was out of shock and confusion that she made it so easy for Dad to get a divorce. Her lawyer wanted her to fight, yet she had no fight left after spending twenty years putting up with Dad's abuse.

She wore a scar above her eyebrow, gifted from Dad during one of his drunken outbursts. It was a common occurrence for him to demand his dinner served to him after neglecting his homelife for weeks at a time.

When we were teenagers, Jimmy was taking archery lessons, and one fateful afternoon, Dad came home drunk and picked a fight with Mom. By now, we were old enough to step in. We had a plan. Jimmy stood poised in the kitchen doorway with bow and arrow drawn and pointed toward Dad. Mom and Dad were hollering at each other; Blaine was perched on the pathway between the hedges that led to our neighbour's house. I stood at the door of our neighbours, waiting for the signal. If Dad laid a hand on Mom, Jimmy would shoot him in the leg, call to Blaine, who would signal me to call the police. Thank God it didn't come to that.

These were the moments that bonded us as siblings. We didn't have "normal" family dinners, sharing stories or talking about our day. Instead, attempting to get Dad's attention with his head buried in the newspaper, Mom grabbed a lighter and set the centre of the paper on fire. It worked, he listened. Our home was dysfunctional and chaotic, but we had each other, and somehow, we managed to pull enough good and identify our common ground so in time, we could look back and reminisce on the crazy antics we dreamt up for the sake of survival.

I don't remember the move, but there I was, living in the big city with my mom and sister. My oldest brother went off to military college in the east, and the other stayed with Dad and they worked together in Dad's machine shop.

Mom enrolled me in Grade 10 at one of the largest schools in the city; It was terrifying. Each day, I would walk in the doors and watch hundreds of students scurrying from class to class like ants. I didn't know a soul. My life was upside-down; My parents split without an explanation, and I was uprooted from my small town and expected just to fit in. Well, I did, but not with the right people. I chose the lifestyle I knew, and school hours were spent everywhere else but on school grounds. That regular three-month assessment came up, and I was escorted out, once again. They didn't need anyone's permission the second time.

While my mom was trying to keep her head above water and navigate the new life she didn't ask for along with the responsibilities of two daughters and a new job, I was trying to party as much as possible, so I didn't have to be home, and I didn't have to think. I had no clue what was going on, but I knew how much pain there was in loneliness.

Mom got my grandma involved when she couldn't deal with me any longer. Grandma lived alone for many years after her husband died in a shooting accident when my mom was eighteen years old. Grandma was a chef at a children's detention centre and told me repeatedly that I would end up in there if I didn't smarten up.

We weren't close by any stretch, and when I reflect, I can only assume she resented me for not supporting *her* daughter by being a good daughter. If that was true, now, as a mother myself, I get it. But back then, there was another side, my side, and my side stayed buried for years before I began to figure things out. I had no foundation on pretty much anything in life. How was I supposed to comprehend anyone else's situation when I didn't have a clue what was going on with my own?

Communication was prohibited in our family. There was never a word spoken. I had no idea what Mom was going through after she and Dad separated and finally divorced. It wasn't until years later that we talked, and I heard her story. I am a mother, and now a grandmother, and I understand Grandma protecting her daughter if that is what she was doing. I like to think it was because of my actions and not because she didn't like me as a person.

Grandma married Uncle Norman when I was fourteen, and though he became our grandfather through marriage, he was an uncle first, from my mom's side. To avoid having to explain to others our family tree that resembles a twisted Juniper in the Arizona desert, I referred to Uncle Norman as my grandpa. As an insider, we called him Uncle Norman.

Grandma was poised and polished. She wore lipstick almost to the day she died at ninety-six years old. Her hair was always perfect, she wore her pearls and earrings daily, and when we visited, she was always sporting a pretty apron. We became accustomed to professionally presented meals, and my mother created the same, because Grandma taught her. Every dish presented was as visually appealing as it was delicious. A dab of melting butter highlighted the mound of green peas accompanied by pearl onions, simple and beautiful in a decorative serving bowl. Mashed potatoes, whipped to perfection, and thin slices of medium-rare roast beef, fanned across the serving platter and garnished with slices of orange for a splash of colour. And the gravy! A feast for the eyes and a tastebud extravaganza.

When we arrived for dinner, the first smell greeting us at the door were the pies she'd made before she made dinner, pastries so delicate and flakey; And she cut triangles from the leftover dough, golden brown with sprinkles of cinnamon and sugar, that we could sample before dinner. It took me years to make a pie that was remotely comparable. Her culinary skills were passed down to my mom, who passed it on to us kids in varying degrees, with Blaine standing head and shoulders above the rest of us.

One day, Grandma marched me into a restaurant to apply for a job, and she was determined this was happening—I wasn't going to waste away, kill myself with drugs, or end up at the serving line in the youth detention centre where she worked. Grandma and I slid into a booth at a family restaurant, and Sam, the manager, sat with us to talk. I am sure Grandma called ahead to pre-pave our meeting and give him a little background on me (and permission to do what was necessary to whip me into shape). He hired me, and I started the next day.

I fell in line under Sam's dictatorship; He was a hard-ass boss from day one. It was strange to learn he was a pastor prior to his restaurant manager position. He was firm but kind, and he trained me to respect the position as a server. We were there to serve, and once I got the hang of it, I enjoyed the rhythm, dancing between tables with the coffee pot, teasing customers with the homemade dessert of the day. This was my day job, and I was earning a paycheque; And the tips ensured I always had cash in my pocket, reserved for the nearby bar where my co-workers knew the bouncers, who turned a blind eye when I walked through the door, knowing full well I was not of legal age to drink.

After a long day at work, my mom would come home to find me with my new friends hanging out in the living room. I didn't do a thing to help her at home. I was one of those useless teenagers no adult wants around, and I didn't know, nor did I know to ask her about how she was doing with the divorce or her new job. She was doing her best to get my sister adjusted to this new life in her new school, and Mom did the best thing she could have done for herself, but more so for me when she handed me a bag of clothes and told me to leave.

I was on my own at sixteen years old. A co-worker offered me a place to stay, and I accepted. This was the start of my real education with hands-on practical lessons, such as Life Skills 101, Treating Others with Compassion, Escaping Emotional Quicksand 101, 102, 201, 202, and Self-Reliance Mastery. As I stepped into my new life, it wasn't long until I realized our crazy dysfunctional family life growing up was paradise compared to what I was moving into.

A SLICE OF HUMBLE PIE

Walking into Maureen's apartment was unnerving. There were toys scattered across the parquet flooring, collecting layers of dog hair and dust bunnies, rolling like tumbleweeds, and wrapping around each chair leg in the kitchen or hiding in the only corner that was visible. The others were shielded behind heaps of clothing, more toys, and a few unidentifiable items. I immediately felt like I needed a shower.

Maureen motioned for me to follow her down the dingy hallway, past the only bathroom, two bedrooms—one was hers on the left, and the other was shared by her three kids on the right—until we walked to the end of the hallway to the last bedroom on the left; This would be my new home.

Oh my God. What am I going to do? I asked myself.

I came from a dust-free home which smelled sweet and looked immaculate most of the time. When Mom had a sewing project on the go, there was cut fabric and the odd pin waiting on the floor in the dining room for Dad to step on. He was usually the one to find them, yelping and cursing and sending Mom scurrying on her hands and knees to collect any strays that might jump up and stab him again.

Within the course of a year, I moved from my comfortable bedroom on the acreage to a townhouse in the big city with Mom and my sister, and now I was reduced to slum conditions with a torn mattress sitting on the floor with no box spring or legs, and kids' underwear, broken toys, and an unused diaper littering the path to the closet.

Well, at least the diaper isn't used, I thought to myself, searching for anything positive to hang onto.

Maureen gestured to the closet door. She turned to me and paused. "Are you ok?" she asked, reading my expression and silence as disapproval. "If this isn't good enough for . . ." she began.

I interrupted and shook my head apologetically. "This is fine, Maureen; I'm sorry. I'm just exhausted," I lied.

This is horrible, I thought, *beyond horrible. How can people live like this?* My thoughts were in complete contrast to what came from my mouth.

"Ok, just checking," she replied and continued with the grand tour.

She opened the closet to a few bent wire clothing hangers dangling from a piece of twine and pulled taught, where a rod may have lived at one point. The top shelf was filled with unidentified objects of every shape and texture, jammed in and ready to burst into the room with the slightest disturbance.

The floor was clear of "stuff," except for more dust bunnies wrapped in dog hair attempting to hide the black build-up of grime along the baseboards.

"I hope this is enough room for your stuff. When Keith and the kids come home, I'll cook dinner. You can join us tonight, but you should get your own food; We can't afford to feed you too."

I felt like such a loser. "Do you have sheets and blanket for the bed, maybe a pillow?" I inquired hopelessly.

Maureen rustled through a storage closet in her bedroom and returned with a sleeping bag and a stained pillow without a pillowcase.

"Sorry, we don't have sheets, but this should work." Half joking, as she tossed everything on the bed and left the room, she flung her overgrown blonde bangs from her face, grinned, and said, "In case you didn't notice, this isn't Snob Hill."

You got that right, I thought to myself. I wrestled with feeling bad for judging this family I moved in with and the standards I didn't realize I had, standards set by my mother. I tried to be gracious and grateful for the roof Maureen had given me but couldn't help thinking that I was so much better than this. *Maybe I am a snob.* The "I'm better than you" judgement I made was a good feeling. It made me feel superior and it warmed me up, tickled my pride a little, and I felt taller, even for just that moment.

I refocused my attention to: I need a plan. How was I going to get out of here? First, I had to accept what was happening, and I remembered Dad's serenity prayer: *accept the things I cannot change.* There was no point in brooding; I couldn't change them, but I could change my situation. I took inventory, a page from my mom's book on survival.

When it came time to plan a grocery trip to town, Mom took inventory of everything she had in the cupboards and fridge, and she created a meal plan to save money on groceries. Blaine and I would take this opportunity to go shopping with her. We were disguised as helpers, but we had an agenda. Maduke Foods was the largest grocery store in town, owned and operated by Mr. Maduke himself. We could see him and his greased-back dark hair with a tinge of grey on the sides, horn-rimmed black glasses, a white shirt and black tie under a sparkling clean apron. He was always running. *How could he stay clean when he was so busy?* I wondered.

Any white shirt I've ever owned had invisible magnets sewn in, attracting anything made with tomatoes.

We followed Mom into Maduke Foods, and when she went left, we took a sharp right toward the cartons of cigarettes piled from floor to ceiling.

We went to town at least once a month, and every time, Blaine and I would each grab a carton of cigarettes, zipping out to the car and hiding them in the back seat. It's not like we needed to do this. After all, we snuck Mom's smokes all the time. We did it for the rush of maybe getting caught. The cigarette heists ended when Mr. Maduke re-merchandised his store and put the cartons in a locked cage, likely realizing his cigarette profits were not what they should have been.

We had a credit account at Maduke Foods. One month, Dad hadn't paid the bill, and Mr. Maduke approached Mom to let her know we were overdue, then announced over the intercom to the staff at the front and anyone else in the store shopping, "No more credit to the Madsens."

That would have been so awful for Mom, enduring the stares from familiar faces as she walked empty-handed from the store to the car. I wondered if she felt as I was feeling as I spread the sleeping bag across the torn mattress, placing one of my shirts over the stained pillowcase to create a barrier between my ear and whatever was living in the pillow. I was humiliated, in a filthy three-bedroom apartment with a co-worker I barely knew and living conditions that couldn't be further from my norm.

I laid down and thought about what I had to work with. I had a job, thanks to Grandma, so I was making money; And I was learning the ropes as a waitress quickly, so tips were growing to line my empty pockets—if I didn't spend them all at the bar— and I could afford incidentals like my own cigarettes. Working the evening shift from 3:00 p.m. to 11:00 p.m. meant I only had to be at the apartment to sleep.

I thought about talks with my dad. A reassuring sensation settled in me: *This is God's will*, I reminded myself. *It is happening for a reason. God has a plan*, I repeated over and over.

Even though I blew it twice in high school, someone in the restaurant told me I could take part-time classes to earn my high school diploma while I worked evenings. This was a perfect solution to avoid the apartment and maybe earn back a little respect from my mom. We hadn't talked in quite some time.

I enrolled in Grade 10 for losers, as we called it. While living at Maureen's, I took math and accounting, doing better than I thought at both. I earned credits in two levels of accounting and managed to pass my first level of math by a slim margin. The hieroglyphics that were foreign to me the day Dad pulled me from school seemed to speak to me this time around.

One afternoon, I went to work to discover we had a new manager; Sam had left with no warning. I was given the night off, and I showed up unexpectedly at the apartment. I could hear Maureen's kids in their bedroom; It sounded like all three of them were in there, but there were no adults to be seen. As I entered the hall, I almost walked into the skipping rope with one end tied tightly around the doorknob of the kids' room and pulled taught across the hallway with the other end tied tightly around the bathroom doorknob. The kids were prisoners in their room.

I quickly untied the skipping rope and opened the door to three kids and the dog on the only bed, a double mattress on the floor with no legs, just like in my rental room. The smell took my breath away; The two-year-old had only a diaper that drooped to her knees, filled with whatever it was that permeated my nostrils. The other two kids, five and seven years old, were sitting cross-legged, their eyes covered with overgrown greasy blonde wispy hair. Food and dirt covered their little faces, and as I looked around the room, they pushed handfuls of cheezies into their mouths.

I asked them where their mom was, and they didn't know. When I pried a little more, I learned this was a regular occurrence. When Maureen came home with her creepy boyfriend, I asked her about it. She told me they couldn't find a sitter and wanted to go out, and she deserved a night out once in a while.

My shifts were all over the place as the new manager was training. I came home to similar episodes with the three kids more often, but the last straw was walking in to find Maureen and her boyfriend on the couch having sex in front of her children.

I almost threw up, and I screamed, "WHAT THE FUCK IS THE MATTER WITH YOU PEOPLE?" and then I ran out the front door.

While growing up, our lives may have been dysfunctional and at times chaotic, but nothing could have prepared me for this. I left that night, leaving my belongings behind. I didn't have a place to go. I didn't own a car. I didn't have a credit card to rent a motel—not that any motel would allow a seventeen-year-old a room to herself. I thought about God's will, and I talked to God, asking for a sign for my next step. I didn't know what to do. It was the wee hours of the morning, and when I stopped walking, I laid down on a bus bench and fell asleep.

GIVE IT TO GORD!

Sam, our former manager, had a nervous breakdown. I had been working mornings since he left and getting to know the new manager, Tim. He was a tall Ukrainian man, big in stature and presence with thick dark brown hair, brown eyes, and a mustache, Tom Selleck style. He was somewhat of a mystery man, but I liked him. In time, he had one brother out of three working as a kitchen manager, and his mother doing prep and making the new lineup of delicious homemade pies and cinnamon buns. Word of her creations quickly spread. They introduced Ukrainian Thursdays, appropriate for the neighbourhood with an abundance of Ukrainian families.

The morning after my night as a homeless person sleeping on the bus bench, I went into work, dreading the hour Maureen was scheduled to work. Tim approached me in the back before my shift and asked why I looked like I pulled an all-nighter. I had no intention of telling anyone what had happened the night before. I was still in shock, and it seemed as though I was surrounded by either Tim's family or Maureen's. Her entire family—brother, mother, father, two sisters and their kids—came into the restaurant every day for two-hour sessions, at least once a day. On occasion, they were there three times a day drinking coffee.

What the hell is wrong with any of these people? They didn't work. They lived behind the restaurant; Hillbilly Central is what I called it, and the mother was the hillbilly matriarch. This is by no means a slight to anyone named Billy living in the hills, only a stereotype I learned from my dad.

Responding to Tim's observation of my unkempt self, I shrugged and told him I wasn't feeling great, but I would work my shift. A group of customers came in and sat at their regular table. They had become as close to friends as I could have had at the time. As I poured their coffee, we chatted and exchanged small talk.

When they asked how my new place was, I cleared my throat and leaned in to tell them, "I need a place to live and fast. I have no place to go after my shift."

The words barely left my mouth when a voice behind me whispered, "You can stay with me."

I turned to find a woman, maybe twenty years older than me, sitting by herself nursing her coffee.

"Hi, my name is Gina Golden. I live in an apartment across from the mall. I live alone with my son, and I have an extra bedroom if you need a place."

I must have stared at her for a minute or two, confused as to what just happened.

"Think about it. Come by after your shift if you would like to look. Here's my address."

She passed me a folded piece of paper, finished her coffee, and told me to have a good day and not to worry as everything was going to be all right.

All day I thought, *should I or shouldn't I?* Then I remembered that things happen for a reason. Dad's voice was inside my head saying, "Give it to God." This was famous saying which my sister and I would later spin into "Give it to Gord."

After work, I walked over to the address Gina had given me. She was on the main floor of the four-story walk-up; Her patio doors faced the main road, and she was sitting in a lawn chair outside with a coffee in hand. She saw me coming, smiled, and gestured to come in. I walked across the lawn and followed her through the patio doors.

"Have a chair. Would you like a coffee?"

I nodded and followed her into the kitchen. She was a slender woman, beautiful for her age, blonde hair cut short around her ears, her blue eyes twinkled kindness, her voice raspy from smoking.

After a good long visit, I took her up on her offer, went over and picked up my meagre belongings from Maureen's. She wasn't home, but her creepy boyfriend was watching TV on the couch. He had on a pair of jeans and no shirt, a beer in one hand and a cigarette in the other. No words were passed between us; I quickly grabbed my things and left.

Over time, I revealed to Gina what had happened. She encouraged me to write an anonymous letter to child services, agreeing that the kids needed protection. Gina said they were probably past the point of repair, but it's the right thing to do. So, I sat down one afternoon and wrote a twelve-page letter detailing all I had seen and experienced first-hand.

The day came when the gossip began; Maureen's mother told me some asshole had reported Maureen. I reacted with shock and asked what had happened. Social services interviewed her and her creepy boyfriend. That's where it ended. They closed the case, and no action was taken. I was mortified, in silence, of course, never revealing that I was the snitch who reported them. I laid awake that night and the next, wondering what would come of those poor kids.

Weeks and months passed, and I still hadn't talked to my mom, but I missed her and reached out with a phone call.

"Hi, Mom, just calling to say hi; I miss you."

"Are you on something?" Her reaction cut deep.

"No, I'm at work; I'll talk to you some other time." I hung up.

I talked to Gina about it later that day. She explained that my mom was at the stage in her life that she didn't need to bend or make concessions for me. If I wanted a relationship with my mom, I would have to make the first move.

I was enrolled in drawing classes and loved it. I had to put High School for Losers on hold for a while; I couldn't keep up the pace of both working and school with all that was going on. The art classes were perfect. I felt at home, and practicing my new sketching techniques took me away from the world, the restaurant, Maureen and her kids, and my strained mother-daughter relationship. The art took me back to class with Mrs. Hatridge, where praise and support fed my soul and made me feel like I had something that no one could take away.

I believed in my heart that I was destined for something big. I felt superior to Maureen's family and the other regulars that hung out in the restaurant with no life to live. I silently judged them all and measured them by what they did or didn't do, how they dressed, how they talked, and what they talked about. In my mind, at the age of seventeen, I figured I had all the answers. Each day, I wondered what I would be guided to next. I was confident that God had another plan for me. I enjoyed being a waitress, but I felt there was more for me. The regulars called me Smiley and I was good at my job. Tim gave me a raise; I was the highest-paid waitress at $6 an hour. I had money, and it was time to get my place.

I found an apartment across the road from Gina. A second-story place with brown carpeting, a balcony facing the main street, and with my very own appliances.

I chose the most eclectic set of living room furniture the Brick had available; Easy, no-interest financing for eighteen months, explained the salesman. I didn't know how interest worked, and 24% sounded reasonable. He cautioned me on what would happen if I didn't pay it before the end of the term, and I appreciated his stern warning when it came time to make my final payment, and I learned how much it would have cost me if I was late. It's too easy for young people to obtain credit without any knowledge or money management skills; I was one of the fortunate ones because I was willing to listen and learn. The salesman further explained how I would build my credit history as I paid it off.

When the furniture truck pulled up, I felt like a grown-up, and they hauled box after box up three flights of stairs to my suite, #315. I unpacked my new TV and stereo system and pulled the cardboard away from the dining room table and its chairs' bamboo legs, and matching couch, chair, coffee, and end tables. As I lifted the cushions from the final box, the bold tropical design with large green leaves, bird-of-paradise, and hibiscus seemed much louder in my apartment than on the showroom floor.

Dad called to tell me he'd sold the acreage. He announced that he and Ricki, his new wife, were moving to PEI. On our last visit before he left, he saw my apartment, and we had dinner together. I was angry he'd decided to move so far away. He assured me if it was meant to be, it would all work out, referring to my situation as well as his own. I found myself justifying every incident in life with Dad's code, It's God's Will, opening myself up to predators; I was a beacon, vulnerable and naive.

My apartment was a few blocks from the restaurant, and I was still working evenings, my shift ending at 11:00 p.m. On a chilly walk home one night, a regular customer drove up, rolled down his window, and asked if I'd like a lift. I was reluctant *(listen to the voice, listen to the voice . . . that voice is your all-knowing self, and your all-knowing self is telling the truth)*.

He suggested I warm up in his car on the ride, and I accepted.

I hopped in the front seat, closed the door, and gave him my address, less than a five-minute drive from the restaurant.

As he pulled away, he asked, "Do you want to see a store I just bought? I am renovating it, and I'd like your opinion."

I agreed, and we took a turn south; Very little was said between us before we arrived at a strip mall. I didn't know this place. He pulled up in front of the end unit with brown paper covering the dirty windows and glass door.

I was trying to act brave, but inside, I was terrified. I didn't know where I was or what would be behind that paper-covered glass. He held the door open; I walked inside. My heart was racing, and now I knew this was bad. Why didn't I run? Why didn't I fight? The light from the lampposts outside streamed between the breaks in the brown paper, and I could see his face above me. He was in his fifties, a day of stubble looked like dirt on his usual clean-shaven face, his dimples dug deep in his cheeks as he grinned. He unbuckled his pants and told me I had to pay for my ride home.

"There are no free rides in this life."

The shame glued so tightly to my chest from the inside, I couldn't tell anyone what had happened. I dreaded the thought of that horrible man coming back to the restaurant; Each time the front door opened, I'd spin around to see if it was him. He never came back.

I tormented myself for months, questioning why I didn't run or fight? The only explanation I could come up with was it was God's will, and there must be a lesson I needed to learn from this. In time, I pushed the memory and shame far deep into the recesses of my mind, almost convincing myself that it never happened.

The restaurant was my security landing pad. I had been waitressing for more than a year when Tim took over as manager. His entire family eventually came to work there; His mother was prepping and cooking, his two brothers were short-order cooks, and his sister joined the front-end as a waitress.

I was sad to see Sam go, especially when I heard he had a nervous breakdown, and I hoped I hadn't been a contributing factor by performing antics with the other servers, like spraying each other with whipped cream balms or throwing tomatoes at the cooks in the back. This reminded me of the bus driver we had when I was young.

Everybody loved Mr. Schmidt, not only was he a skilled bus driver, but he was also fearless. It didn't matter the weather; It was playtime for him when other drivers cancelled on blizzardy winter mornings. A four-foot drift across the road was a challenge for this superhero behind the wheel.

Hollering to the back of the bus, "Hold on!" his foot pressed hard on the gas pedal, he rammed head-on, nailing the wall of cemented snow, digging deep with his cheering fans at his back, screaming, "Go, go, go!" On the odd occasion, the bus would spin, pushing the rear end sideways, and we'd come to a stop. There was always a farmer close by with a tractor to save us, and school would have to wait for the storm to pass; Mr. Schmidt, slightly deflated, took each of us home.

I stood at the mailbox for my first day of school in Grade 9, expecting Mr. Schmidt to be smiling back at me as the bus door flung open to an unfamiliar, sombre man sitting in Mr. Schmidt's seat.

"Where's Mr. Schmidt?" each of us asked as we climbed the steps.

"Retired," is all he said, and the door slammed shut behind each of us.

We were heartbroken and resentful; Mr. Schmidt didn't warn us, as he hadn't said anything about retiring. He just left without a word, and this imposter took over. We were not kind to our new driver, not in the least, and we made Mr. Carter's life a living hell for the first three months of his new job, thinking he would quit, and Mr. Schmidt would return.

We threw Oreo cookies at the back of his head, made rude remarks, and smoked cigarettes in the back seats. One morning, we told him one of the parents had called and asked us to inform the bus driver their child wouldn't be going to school that day. The anticipation of our prank was satisfied as we watched the girl running to the end of her driveway, waving her arms, and throwing her lunch box to the ground as we drove by at full speed. Mr. Carter came to the house that night to tell Mom what we were doing.

I knew Mr. Carter from my school. He was the invisible janitor I'd pass in the hall. He never looked up or engaged with any students; He focused on his task at hand, washing or waxing the long hallway floors.

When it clicked and we connected the bus driver as the janitor, it didn't take long to figure out how to torment him in the school. If he quit the janitor position, we assumed he would also leave the driving job, and Mr. Schmidt would be back.

When he left the mop and bucket unattended, we'd sneak over, upend the bucket, flooding the floors with soapy water. This continued until I was caught and sent to the library for a strap.

Christmas was nearing, and I volunteered to collect money from everyone on the bus to buy our new driver a Christmas present. I put little thought into the gift, as I assumed by shows I watched on TV that the appropriate gift would be chocolates and a bottle of wine.

The day before we broke for Christmas, Mom reluctantly picked up the wine for me; She didn't think the wine was appropriate as a gift from a group of kids. I was just eager to get it over with, wondering why I volunteered in the first place.

Mom found Mr. Carter's address in the phone book and took my brother and me to his house after dinner. He, too, lived in the country, not far from us. We turned into his neatly plowed driveway. Evergreen trees reached into the sky on both sides, blocking out what little daylight remained, and then we saw it.

The door hung between patchwork plywood walls in assorted colours and shapes, with a tin roof bent roughly over the walls on all three sides to keep the moisture out.

Blaine and I gasped. Every Oreo cookie, rude remark, bucket of water, and horrible gesture flooded my mind, and the tears welled in my eyes. We looked at each other, and I knew Blaine was thinking the same thing; We were monsters.

I felt the heat on my face, and my heart pounded as we walked to the door and knocked. Slivers of amber light peaked through the door board seams, and rusty hinges gently squeaked as Mr. Carter appeared. He had a warm smile and kind eyes I hadn't seen until now. The oil lamp backlit his tall, slender stature, and six children and his wife were seated, patiently waiting to return to their interrupted dinner.

Mr. Carter invited us in; We gently wiggled the door closed behind us, nudging it back in its hole. A wood stove crackled in the corner. I had a compulsion to flee. Instead, we stood at the doorway, staring at this family who were smiling back at us.

Their house was no more than a shack, with no electricity, and I assumed later, their water supply was likely drawn from a hand pump.

"Sorry for interrupting your dinner." This was the kindest thing I had ever muttered to this man. "We have a gift for you from all the kids on the bus. Merry Christmas."

I scanned the room for signs of the holidays, and there were none: no Christmas tree, no lights, not even a wreath on the door. Mr. Carter thanked us as he took the box of chocolates.

"We don't drink alcohol, but we will certainly enjoy the chocolates. Thank you again."

He asked us to regift the wine and promptly introduced us to each of his children and Mrs. Carter, and she asked if we had eaten dinner. We assured them we had.

They were poor yet willing to share their meal with us. How could they be so lovely to us when we had been so awful, tormenting this man daily? I assumed he was a grumpy old janitor, never looking past the mop and bucket. He stole Mr. Schmidt's job; That was all I saw until we stood in his home.

The pit in my stomach was growing by the second, pushing its way up through my chest, threatening to burst from the shame and guilt flooding my insides; My ears pounded in time with my heart, and I wanted to throw up.

"We have to go," I muttered, swinging around and bolting out the door to Mom's car, where I lost it and burst into uncontrollable sobs.

I thought about Mr. Carter every day through the holidays, wondering how he must have felt, putting up with our antics when all he was trying to do was work his two jobs to support his family. We learned later that Mr. Carter was a religious man, and so he didn't drink alcohol, nor did they celebrate Christmas in the same way we did. I knew nothing of this man before our trip up his driveway.

I knew why I felt compelled to co-ordinate the gift from a bus full of kids to our driver. I was to be taught the lesson of empathy and kindness, and from that day on, I intentionally shared my lesson with Mr. Carter. I brought him homemade cookies I snuck from the cookie jar. I wished him a good morning and a good night as the bus door folded open, and I sprinted down the steps, turning to wave. I stood up to the other kids who picked on the invisible janitor at my school. He was no longer invisible to me.

Tim was making changes in the restaurant and transferred me to the sister restaurant downtown with my buddy Steven. It was to be a temporary move as they shuffled staff around. I didn't like the downtown location. Men in suits came in for lunch and thought nothing of whistling for my attention or grabbing my ass when I walked by. When I told Tim, he told me it was because I was so good at what I did and encouraged me to be nice to them. "The client is always right" was his mantra.

On one afternoon, when Steven and I were left to close for the night, and while he cashed out, I finished cleaning up and joined him in the front while he counted the daily cash. We were chatting as I walked by and stood against the glass display case that housed all the desserts. Steven's back was to me as we talked. When I placed my hands behind and on top of the glass display to hoist myself to sit on the case, the unsecured glass slid out from under me, and I fell backward through the glass display and onto the floor, spewing broken glass and blood in all directions.

"Steven, check my back, check my back!" I hollered to him as he panicked, running back and forth in shock, unsure of what to do next.

He checked behind me, no cuts on my back. He grabbed a towel to wrap around my torn arm, the blood hitting the floor in a steady stream. Steven called the ambulance and held my arm tight.

I lost consciousness in the ambulance a few times as they pulled me from the back door into the emergency room; Steven stayed behind, trying to clean my blood from the floor of the ambulance.

Steven was my best friend, supervisor, and trainer. He knew the restaurant business well, and Tim gave him a great deal of responsibility between both locations. He was good at his job, but many people misunderstood him.

He was a slight young man with blonde hair and delicate features. He hustled through the rows of tables, smiling, flicking his hair like a schoolgirl, and when he was stressed or flustered in the least, his cheeks flushed a brilliant pink. His father was a poised and proper man and worked in a high-end men's clothing store as a sales manager, and as a result, Steven was well-dressed.

Many people thought Steven was gay. His gestures were feminine, and he had a high-pitched voice, and he was teased for his emphasized and elongated *s*'s. I believed he was gay until I met his girlfriend, and I didn't care either way. The one time we talked about it, I knew by his reaction to the topic that he was deeply bothered by people's assumptions and reactions. I had no idea how deeply he was affected until after my accident.

I was shoved in the hallway of the chaotic hospital, awaiting preoperative measures. There was a nursing strike, and they were highly short-staffed. An intern came by and asked if I needed anything.

"I'd love a cigarette."

"I'll see what I can do." The intern came back with a bedpan for a makeshift ashtray and lit my cigarette for me.

Yes, we could smoke everywhere back then.

My whole body began shaking violently. I had lost so much blood that the rush of smoke sent me into convulsions. A passing doctor grabbed my cigarette, scolding the intern, and demanded I be taken into the operating room instantly. They whisked me off. That's one sure way to get pushed to the front line. I woke up in a room with my mom and my new stepfather sitting beside the bed.

My arm was completely bandaged. I was relieved to see my mom sitting there. The glass cut through the inside of my left upper arm and forearm, missing an artery by millimetres. I was lucky but out of commission for a while. I was more upset about having to cut my art classes. This was my dominant arm, and they didn't know how much long-term damage there may be.

While recovering, a night on the town with Steven seemed like a good idea. I made a sling with a fabric colour to match my outfit, and off we went to the Rose and Crown Pub. We separated at some point in the evening, and a couple offered to drive me home.

The next day, I went to the restaurant to see how Steven made out with a ride. We went outside so no one could listen in, and he told me of his horrific night: A man had offered to drive him home, and he'd raped Steven.

The guilt was so heavy; I felt wholly responsible for what had happened to Steven. I had left him, and we should never have split up that night. He never really sprung back to his jovial self. He left the restaurant, and we lost touch over time.

A few years later, I ran into his father and asked how Steven was doing. He hung his head as he told me that Steven had taken his life.

I couldn't speak. I didn't know what to say, and that familiar guilt flooded back. How could this have happened? Was it because of that horrible night? Was it partially my fault?

After speaking with a few friends, I agreed that his death was his release from pain. I recalled my intuition when I first met him; I knew he was gay, and I didn't care. I loved Steven for who he was.

That era was horrible for homosexuals, and I knew people who hid their true selves behind heterosexual relationships in fear of persecution. I was certain Steven's death resulted from the pain of living dual lives and masking his truth to preserve his image. RIP, my friend.

GINA, THE OUIJA, AND MY BOYFRIEND

After six weeks off, I went back to my original position, never returning to the downtown location. I was back on the evening shift and serving my old regulars again. There was an older couple I grew fond of. They came in regularly after dinner; He ordered a coffee for himself and a pot of hot water for her. She brought her tea bag every time. Occasionally, they would share a cinnamon roll after I sold them on how incredible they were when sliced in half like a bun, and then buttered and grilled. They grew fond of me too, fond enough to want to introduce me to their son.

They came in one evening with not only their son but his sister, brother, and cousins. The minute we looked at each other, I figured they had told him about me. His warm, trusting smile, stretched between earlobes, was tucked under a thick black mustache. He was beyond cute.

I saw they had their drinks and had been taken care of by one of the other servers. I figured out the best way to introduce myself was the direct approach since his parents were playing matchmaker, and we both knew it. I walked to their table, acknowledged the parents, who introduced their guests and finished with their son, Kelly—openly reminding me they were bringing him in to meet me. Awkwardly and a little embarrassed by their public matchmaking, I reached out to shake his hand, engaging with his larger-than-life smile and sparkly brown eyes; I felt a rush of heat surround the mammoth butterflies pushing up against my diaphragm. His perma-smile triggered my heart rate, and my flushed cheeks were a sure giveaway; I was smitten.

A few days later, he returned without his parents and asked me out.

We dated for several months. On my days off, I joined him on road trips, learning not to wear shoes in the cab of his Peterbilt truck or eat anything that might shed a crumb or two. We stopped for meals in restaurants or a washroom break much more often than he was used to. He watched as I opened the passenger door, swung my legs around to slip my shoes on without touching the floor, and he called me peanut bladder each time I descended the steps to skip toward the public washrooms and sneak a cigarette along the way.

He had planned a trip to Europe with his family long before we met and asked if I would house-sit for him while they were gone. His bungalow had pristinely manicured grass and was sparsely furnished inside, with car magazines decorating the corners, nightstands, and side tables in the living room. I learned shortly before he left for his trip that he had been married before, and his ex-wife had taken most of the furniture, leaving him with a lamp and the sofa.

Gina remained a fixture in my life while I was dating Kelly. I babysat her son when she was off doing whatever she did. She didn't have a job, and it was her son who told me their only source of income was government assistance. I was her source of cigarettes, a habit we shared with pots of coffee and a Ouija board she constructed from scrabble pieces. When she introduced me to her board, I was intrigued and scared since my mom had told us stories about her experiences when she and her sister bought a store version of Ouija. After months of nightmares and strange things happening in the house, a psychic had told my mom to burn the board.

Gina knew I had been on a quest to understand my connection with God. She tied her obsession with her board with my desire to discover my spiritual roots, assuring me the board was safe if it was treated respectfully. My curiosity and desire to learn as much as I could about all things spiritual kept me coming back to Gina's house, the board, and her daily tarot card readings.

In the centre of her kitchen table, scrabble pieces formed a circle with the letters from A to Z and the numbers from one to nine; A handwritten zero was drawn on the face of a blank scrabble piece, along with a scrabble piece for YES and another for NO. With a shot glass upside down in the middle of the circle, we each rested two fingers gently on the top and waited.

The glass would slowly move from letter to letter, either spelling words or just gibberish.

"You're pushing it," I told her often, and she insisted that it was moving on its own.

I was always a little freaked out as we sat down with the board, as she seemed to have a relationship with it and referred to the board as a person or personality.

Testing my skepticism, I would try it on my own as she stood at the kitchen counter making a pot of watered-down coffee. She put two tablespoons of coffee grounds in the machine for twelve cups of water. She said she liked her coffee weak, but I believed her budget was the real reason for the tasteless, transparent attempt. I would often bring her packages of coffee from the restaurant as a gesture of thanks and hoped she'd make a real pot. Instead, she opened the coffee packets, adding them to her coffee can kept fresh in the compartment of the freezer.

The board became an obsession between shifts at the restaurant and time spent with Kelly. I would leave for work early to spend an hour with Gina and the board, asking questions about people we knew or when we would win the lottery. I was so impressionable when it came to spiritual ideas. I believed that each time someone new crossed my path, it was an act of God. Every cell in my body thought God had a plan for me, and my purpose would be revealed at some point along the way. I looked for signs everywhere, always on alert, noticing subtle nuances in words spoken or body language that might deliver the answer to my question, "What is my purpose?"

God kept it from me, and there was a purpose for that too. I had to earn my stripes, and karma would be my facilitator. I had a list of items requiring penance from my childhood, and my purpose would remain hidden from me until the magical moment when the skies would part, and God would send his messenger to deliver my golden egg.

As I sat with Gina at the board one morning, we had our two fingers perched atop the shot glass, and we were waiting. The glass began to move and spelled the words B-E-W-A-R-E — M-A-N — O-U-T-S-I-D-E. Gina stood up and looked out the patio window; No one was there. Shrugging it off, we carried on. That evening, we went for a walk. The streetlamps lit the back alley behind the bar across the street from Gina's apartment. Semi-trucks parked behind the bar parallel to the back alley. As we walked and talked, heading toward the back alley, I caught a glimpse of someone on the other side of the truck. He shifted his feet as we approached the dimly lit back alleyway, sliding behind the wheels and out of sight.

I turned to Gina. "A man is hiding over there."

She grabbed my hand and pulled; We ran as fast as our legs could move, through the alley, circling the block, zigzagging between two houses to the back of her apartment. We went in through the back door of her building. When we were sure there was no one behind us, we snuck back into her apartment and peeked through the curtains toward the street with the semi-truck. It struck us simultaneously; The board gave us that message that morning: *BEWARE MAN OUTSIDE.*

Up to this point, I hadn't bought what Gina was selling by insisting the board was there to protect and guide us. I was convinced she was orchestrating the shot glass. The man behind the truck changed my mind, and I came to realize that there was something to this board thing: unseen forces at work.

My nightmares began while I was house-sitting for Kelly. I was afraid to go to sleep, and the weeks of torturous nightmares as a child returned. My thoughts flashed over every horror film I had watched with my brothers, and the gut-wrenching fear of the presence of evil in the movie *The Exorcist* haunted me. One night, as I laid in bed, still awake with the night-light on, a cool breeze swept under the covers at my feet, lifting the blanket ever so slightly from my calves. There was a presence in the bedroom that night, and I felt something or someone as if a person was sitting next to me. I believed the board was a gateway to my ghostly visitor, and I chose to close the gate and never return to Gina's board.

Was the board God's will too? I wrestled with that for a while, concluding that Gina's fascination with the occult did not align with the spirituality I had come to know and trust. The feeling was too different, but perhaps it was God's will for me to experience it, which proved beneficial years later when I assisted a priest in what I called an exorcism (though Father Thomas reminded me a couple of times, "It was a cleansing, Shauna, not an exorcism.").

BIG NEWS

Shortly after Kelly returned from Europe, we decided it was a good idea for me to move in with him, and I brought my furniture to fill the empty spaces.

I didn't have any depth of knowledge or experience with healthy relationships. I had no idea what I was doing. I was eighteen and Kelly was twenty-seven when we'd begun dating, and we were living together in less than a year. There was never any discussion about the future, what we wanted, how to deal with money, or any serious matters. I had no idea what intimacy meant or how to communicate with a man. We went through the motions of sharing a home; Each of us went to work, came home, and watched TV.

"What's wrong?" was a common question directed to Kelly sitting behind a newspaper or car magazine.

He would fire back with a puzzled expression, "NOTHING," in a tone that turned me inward, and silence became the norm between us.

The familiarity of chaos and excitement for change had me so charged up the day I found out I was pregnant, and I was so eager to share the news with my mom and with Kelly. I was sure my mom would be over the moon, and the big reveal would bring Kelly and me closer and create the connection I craved.

I picked up the phone with butterflies dancing the cha-cha in my diaphragm and blurted out, "Hey, Mom, I have some great news; I am pregnant."

A long pause of piercing silence deflated my enthusiasm, and all she could reply with was "Really?" in a tone of utter disappointment.

The conversation ended quickly. I truly believed this news would be the ticket to a deeper connection with my mom. How could she not be excited? I was over the moon, and I knew in my heart that this was meant to be. This was God at work again in my life, and I had no doubt it was the best thing that could happen.

After a long cry in the kitchen, I assured myself the response from Mom shouldn't have been any different considering the rocky relationship we'd had for the past few years.

When Mom and Dad divorced, Mom went through hell, and I fueled the fires. She put up with so much then, so how could she feel good about my news now? She probably thought I would screw this up too. Gina told me it would take time with Mom.

I was nineteen, pregnant, and a waitress in a family restaurant. I thought I had it all together. I sat in the kitchen waiting for Kelly to come home. He walked through the front door, my butterflies were humming fiercely, and my back tensed as he bent over to kiss me.

"I have some exciting news to tell you; I'm pregnant."

His reaction was so unexpected. He spun around without a word, marched into the bathroom, and closed the door. After several minutes, I realized he was in the bathroom shaving and decided he needed time to process this. After all, it was big news—life-changing for sure—and I was so excited, regardless of anyone else's opinion.

I stared at the bathroom door, waiting. *Oh my God,* I thought to myself. *This is the most extensive shave and shower I've had to endure.*

I just wanted to talk and hug and know he was as happy as I was. The bathroom door opened, and he stood in the doorway glaring intently at me, and without a word, as he finished wiping each ear dry with his towel, he spun around and retreated to the bedroom, disappearing behind the door.

The silence was agonizing and familiar. Whenever I brought up a subject he didn't like, he went silent, never to return to the topic again. The bedroom door opened, and he walked straight to the closet where our coats hung, pulled his jacket out, and glared at me again as he slid each arm in and zipped it up without losing eye contact with me. I didn't know if I should say anything, so I just sat there and stared back as he reached for the doorknob, and out he went, without a word.

I waited at the kitchen table, smoking cigarette after cigarette, flipping through the infant section of the Sears catalogue. I knew this was meant to be. I could feel it as the excitement escalated at the turn of each page. *It's God's will*, I kept assuring myself.

It was three hours before the front door opened, and he stepped through to the very spot he had stood staring at me earlier. Again, he stood for a moment in silence and then said it.

"Get an abortion, or we are done."

His words hung in the air long after he hung his coat and retreated to the bedroom, closing the door behind him. He would be getting up for work in a few hours. At 3:00 a.m., he would leave the house and wouldn't be back for a couple of days, hauling milk products to various locations in the province.

I slept on the couch that night and didn't hear him leave. When I awoke, I called my brother, Blaine, to tell him what had happened and that I had to move out that day. I wasn't waiting another moment. How dare he put himself ahead of a baby. I was so angry. I cried all morning as I packed my clothes. How dare he give me an ultimatum. I would show him! There was no way I would be there when he returned home.

Blaine had to rent a moving van since my driver's licence was less than a year old and I didn't have a credit card. He drove up to the front of the house. I felt pangs of guilt as we loaded my belongings into the truck. Kelly would be left with an empty house, as it was when I moved in. I couldn't bring myself to take my table that replaced the stack of phonebooks his living room lamp sat on when I moved in.

It didn't take long to load what little belongings I had and even quicker to unload into the storage space included with Blaine's two-bedroom townhouse rental. The row of storage units looked identical, each with a roll-top door, sliding up to reveal a dirt floor and less than a hundred square feet of storage space. Being the neat freak that he had always been, my brother kept his treasures neatly stacked against the back wall, leaving me plenty of room for my things.

My pride and anger didn't leave room to question whether I was hasty, or whether Kelly might change his mind after he cooled off. I wrote a note and told him I was going to my brother's. Under the anger and hurt, there was a fairy-tale idea that he would come to his senses, jump on his white horse, scoop me up, and we would live happily ever after. No horse. No scooping. No fairy tale. I didn't hear from him until Erika was born.

When I left the hospital with this bit of a person, Mom came to the rescue, suggesting we stay with her for a while so I could work out the kinks as a new mom, and I didn't hesitate. The time spent with Mom and learning how to care for a newborn was priceless, and it started the lifelong bond between us.

Kelly and I went our separate ways, never finding common ground to build on, likely out of resentment and pride on my side. Our world views were so different; No doubt that raising a child together would not have gone well. Even still, I always looked to the horizon with a glimmer of hope that he would come and rescue us, with Dad's voice in my head saying, "If it's God's will."

Tim called to let me know he was buying a restaurant in a small town three hours west, and he wanted me to come and work for him. He would have a nanny and a place for Erika and me. I would help set up the restaurant's front end, and there would be profit sharing; It all sounded perfect. I was excited to move on to the next adventure, working with Tim and his family and doing what I enjoyed. This could be the ideal stepping stone as I saw myself one day owning my own café or shop. Tim said he always saw me in a shop of my own, too, doing creative things. The idea felt good; I knew God had a plan for us, and helping Tim set up his new restaurant seemed like the right thing to do. I packed up our things, and my eight-month-old daughter and I went off to the armpit of the province.

Everything Tim had promised couldn't have been further from reality. Our living quarters was an old trailer behind the restaurant with no running water, and the resident mice ran up and down behind the walls at night. I had Erika sleeping with me in case one of those nasty rodents jumped in her bed. As for the nanny, I heard day in and day out "She's coming." When she finally arrived, it turned out to be Tim's mother, who was as ancient as the trailer we were living in. So, Erika came to work with me every day and ran around in her walker, entertaining the customers. That was certain to be the most enjoyable time spent in that godforsaken place. Speaking of which, where was God in all this? Indeed, he didn't expect us to live like this.

I learned after we arrived that Tim had taken all the meat from the restaurant he was managing and, during a midnight move, cleaned out the freezer and coolers, stealing from his former boss to stock his new restaurant. I also learned that I would not earn a wage since I had a place to live, and we had food to eat at the restaurant. I was told that any extras I needed could come from my tips. No profit-sharing until there were profits to be had. This opportunity became a nightmare soon after we arrived.

Calling my mother to admit all that had happened was tough. I told her about Tim disappearing on drinking binges, leaving the restaurant without a cook, and I was left alone to cook and serve with Erika at my side. I tried to hold back the emotion, but I let it all out, and through sobs, told Mom about our living conditions: having to bathe Erika in a metal tub behind the restaurant and the smell of the disgusting trailer that Tim said only needed my creative touch to make it more like home. I had no money to come home, and no way to get there. On a hot summer day when the temperature was over 30 degrees Celsius, Mom pulled up in a rental van without air conditioning to rescue Erika and me.

I was defeated, tired, broke, and the only place I knew to go was back to Gina's. Burdening Mom was not in the cards. She had a full-time job, and I didn't want to taint the relationship we were building on. Gina was friends with the property manager of her building, and when she told him about me, he agreed to give us a place for free until I was on my feet.

The winds of change are in control when we give our power away. I gave my power away, trusting that Tim had my back. He was a wolf in sheep's clothing, and I was the prey. When we arrived at Gina's, she introduced me to the property manager, Danny. I was ill-prepared for what I was walking into when I accepted Danny's offer for the free apartment. Predators are attuned to the vulnerabilities of others, picking up quickly on their weaknesses, and I was prime for the picking.

THE MONSTER

I soon learned that the property manager was not all that he seemed. In retrospect, I discovered this too late. I entered into the most dangerous relationship I could ever have imagined. I was drawn to Danny's charming and charismatic personality, and I was lonely. He said all the right things in the beginning, and I took him at his word, and so I opened up, sharing my fears and dreams. Once he knew he had me, his true colours revealed his dark and dangerous side. Erika and I endured months of manipulation and emotional and physical abuse. Danny prayed on weak women, children, and anyone he could control. I wasn't the first woman to experience his dual personality —shifting from charming, witty, and engaging when the persona suited his needs to a violent, cruel, and unpredictable monster. His facial features and demeanour changed to match the level of rage sparked by any action, comment, or response from me, his two boys, or Erika. She wasn't even two years old and posed a threat to him for some reason. He warned me daily that if I contacted authorities or reached out to my family for help, he would kill them, and I had no doubt at the time that he meant it. I toed the line and kept my head down as best I could in fear of triggering the next fit of rage, always on the lookout for a way out.

I was grateful to meet two sisters operating a day home close by. They had moved from Nova Scotia and opened a day home together, offering childcare with flexible hours which was perfect for my 3:00 a.m. shifts at the restaurant where I cooked. Each day after work, I walked to their place to pick Erika up, and they invited me in for coffee and became my lifeline to the outside world. Spending time with them gave me a glimpse into what a happy life could look like for Erika and me. I opened to them about our sheltered life and Danny's abuse, and they assured me that Erika and I would always have a safe place with them. One afternoon after work, as we sipped our coffee at their kitchen table, we watched Erika content and happy, playing with the other children, and they commented on how resilient children can be. I took that moment to tell the sisters that I was pregnant and believed Danny may have replaced my birth control pills with a placebo to make it happen. I hadn't told another soul at this point. I was plotting our escape, one step at a time.

Danny was a regular churchgoer, a "born-again" Christian—part of his facade to the outside world. He believed that his collection of religious symbols was a testament to the outside world of what a great guy he was. Along with the rosary that dangled from the rearview mirror of his dilapidated Peugeot, he hung his poster of Jesus on display in the living room where passersby would see through the undraped picture window. Everything was to disguise the horrific truths inside.

When he discovered I had made friends with the day home sisters, he announced we were moving to a basement suite apartment. I used the move as an excuse to reach out to my mom, convincing him that Erika could stay with her while we moved and settled in. All I could think of was getting my daughter to a safe place. I confessed to Danny's two sons that I was pregnant, and they encouraged me to leave with Erika. His boys were sixteen and fourteen years old at the time, and they confided in me that they too were victims of his physical and sexual abuse.

For the first time, I was on my knees praying, directing my requests to the poster of Jesus on the mantle above the fireplace, pleading with God to help us and save us from this nightmare. Reflecting on the words from both the local pastor and the Catholic priest, with whom I sought advice—"It's a noble thing to stick by him; God would approve"—I asked both leaders how this could be part of God's plan. I wasn't allowed to see my family and friends. Danny abused his boys and almost killed my daughter when he threw her on the floor, splitting her skull from front to back.

I needed a way out. I needed help!

At that moment, the doorbell rang. I was overwhelmed with emotion when I opened the door to see my siblings standing there.

"Something has happened to Mom; You have to come."

I knew in my heart that this was a ploy. I recognized the tone from our childhood when we were plotting to save our mom from our dad. I knew they were there to keep me from the monster asleep in the other room.

Danny heard us talking and bolted from the bedroom and was caught off guard when he saw who stood in the doorway.

I grabbed my purse and said, "I have to go. Something happened to Mom."

"No, you aren't going anywhere." He reached for my arm.

Jim stepped inside, between Danny and me, and insisted, "She's coming with us."

Danny backed away, and we left. In the car, safe and secure, I began to cry; I was safe for the first time in months. We were finally free. We drove to our grandma's, where Erika was staying. The family felt it was safer to have her there if Danny came looking for us.

Two policemen escorted me back to the apartment to collect our belongings and stood at the door while we loaded the truck. By this time, assault charges had been laid against Danny, and he was out on bail. Now I was face to face with the monster, standing in the corner with his arms folded across his chest, his evil demeanour staring back at me. I knew he would have killed me if I hadn't had police officers as my escort on that day.

My dad happened to be visiting from the East Coast during the chaos. I confessed to Dad, my siblings, and my mom about the life we lived before my rescue. After the charges were laid, Danny's former wife came forward and laid assault charges of her own; He was facing fifteen separate charges, including sexual assault against their daughter and assault causing bodily harm against his wife. She thanked me for standing up to him and said she was too scared to initiate any charges on her own. I assured her that I was too scared too; I needed my family to intervene.

The decision was made: We were moving to the East Coast with Dad. My younger sister would use his plane ticket, and we'd meet at the airport in Charlottetown. Dad bought a pickup truck with a canopy, and we loaded what was left of our belongings, said goodbye to the family, and hopped in Dad's truck, filling the cab with snacks and diapers for our 4,700 km trek to the other side of the country. We had to beat the plane my sister was coming in on, so what usually would take several days of driving, we made in two and a half days and caught the last ferry of the day from the mainland to the island. Two and a half days of talking, laughing, and crying together. We stopped only long enough for a bite to eat, bathroom breaks, and food for Erika; Her diapers littered the highway across six provinces.

We were in Ontario, coming up a hill when the ashtray caught on fire, and smoke billowed out the windows. I scrambled to pull the ashtray from the dash and chucked the burning mess out the window, but not before we reached the top of the hill when the gas pedal stuck to the floor, and we were picking up speed quickly.

Dad said, "Look, it's a police car."

At the bottom of the hill, a marked car sat on the shoulder of the road.

"I can't get the gas pedal to . . ."

He pumped repeatedly and turned off the ignition as a last resort. The truck coasted past the police car at a reasonable speed, the ashtray was extinguished, and we pulled over a few hundred metres ahead of what could have been a hefty ticket and a whole lot of explaining. We recapped the experience, laughing in disbelief at how each moment unfolded. Erika slept through the ordeal, curled up on her makeshift bed at my feet.

As we stood on the deck of the ferry, Dad had one arm around my shoulder and held Erika snug in his other.

The sun was settling into the most blissful horizon I had ever seen when Dad squeezed my shoulders and said, "Your new life begins now."

I cried some more, and then more, for days. When we settled in after picking up my sister at the airport, the fear that held me captive for months melted away with every tear of gratitude flowing from an endless reservoir of emotions. We were free.

Long before we left our old life, I decided about the little person growing inside of me, knowing I didn't have the emotional or mental capacity to provide a quality life for two children on my own. I knew there was something to the "God's will" concept my dad built a life on when my siblings appeared at the door at the exact moment I was on my knees, pleading for help. I didn't need any more convincing.

Everything leading up to the moment we stood on the deck of the ferry made sense to me, and I knew the steps to take next. An appointment with a psychiatrist confirmed that psychopaths are the product of their environment. With a violent father and passively drunk mother, the seeds were well-fertilized to develop into the monster Danny became, and I breathed a sigh of relief to learn it was not a genetic issue for the unborn child growing inside of me.

After settling in at Dad's, the second priority was to find out how to go about the adoption process. As a penniless twenty-two-year-old pregnant mother with one still in diapers, I figured social services would be the best place to start.

I sat across the desk of a short, stout man, a dead ringer to a young Danny DeVito. His receding hairline was met with long dark tufts of hair poking above his ears, sprinkling white flecks of dandruff onto the shoulders of his black turtleneck. As he read the lengthy documents I provided, I sat and watched as he nodded, grunted, and proceeded to swirl the eraser end of his pencil around the inside of his nostril. Oh my God, he was picking his nose with his pencil.

I shot up out of my chair, slammed my hands on his desk and hollered, "I wouldn't leave a dead dog with you!"

I stormed out of his office, down the steps, and into Dad's truck.

This was further confirmation that I had divine assistance. Everything that followed being in the nose picker's office had proved to me, without a doubt, that there was a plan. I did have choices, and I had guidance when I stopped long enough to listen and feel.

I took Dad's advice and booked an appointment with a well-respected doctor in the community. He was a family man, with a brood of kids as Dad put it. I think six children would qualify as a brood, and I was shocked to see how young Dr. Blackwood was when he stepped into the examination room.

He was gracious and patient while I told him how I came to be on the island and why I decided to put the baby up for adoption. Rather than judging me—something I half-expected when I learned he was a religious man—he welcomed the idea and asked whether I would consider a private adoption. He knew a couple with their names on a ten-year waiting list to adopt a baby, and if I were open to the idea, he would contact them.

The news came from back home that Danny took a plea deal, agreeing to the conditions set out by the judge. My aunt sat at the back of the courtroom and heard the testimonial from Danny's former wife and my written testimonial read by the prosecutor. Every word pressed deep into the yellow-lined legal pad to release the pain, fear, anger, and the gnawing guilt for putting my little girl through hell. The court and my aunt heard it all.

That monster destroyed lives, and in return, only four of the fifteen charges stuck in exchange for a lifetime restraining order for my family and me, stripped from all parental rights for my unborn child and a four-year sentence in a medium-security prison. The news hit me hard; I so wanted them to lock him in with the murderers and let fate take care of the rest, wiped from the face of the earth at the hands of a different kind of monster, one who looked upon sexual and child abusers as the lowest forms of life unworthy of living.

I sat at Dad's kitchen table, wrapped in the warmth from the fire crackling in the woodstove. Everyone was still asleep; The silence was my morning gift. The windows along the wall of his tiny two-bedroom house stretched from floor to ceiling in the kitchen and along the wall in a three-season sunroom off the living room where my sister was sleeping.

Duke, my former companion, moved to the island with Dad when he sold our acreage in the West, and that dog greeted me like a long-lost friend when I first arrived. By then, he was fifteen years old and arthritis had set in his back legs, but his tail wagged just fine. The island air was good for Duke, and their little house sat on three acres overlooking the bay. *Perfect for a Chesapeake Bay retriever,* I thought, *since he loves to chase birds and scour for treasures along the water's edge.* Every morning, I sat at the kitchen table, watching the waves wash against the red sandy shore, with driftwood scattered amongst the rocks below. I decided this was what heaven looked like, and I was finally at peace.

LITTLE ROSEMARY

Dad and I walked into the restaurant to meet the potential parents of the babe inside me. Their young girl was skipping around the table, whispering a tune to herself as we approached and introduced ourselves. Rudy and Janice glanced at my belly as we exchanged greetings and asked how I was feeling and how far along my pregnancy was.

When I sat, the young girl came to attention beside me with a smile, told me her name, and without hesitation announced, "And I'm adopted."

Learning Rudy was an accountant and Janice was a teacher comforted me instantly; They had the means to give the baby a good life. They explained that they could not have children of their own, and I thought to myself how cruel and unfair it was for two people who want nothing more than to have a baby, in contrast to the people I came to know, who should never have been parents. They shared their adoption story with their three-year-old spitfire skipping around the table as we talked. They'd waited for years when their daughter finally arrived and had been on a waiting list since. A young woman agreed to adoption, only to change her mind after the baby was born; They were devastated. No wonder they seemed guarded as we talked about my plans.

Without sharing my whole story with two strangers, I told them this was my calling, as vital a calling as when I learned I was pregnant with Erika. I knew it was right then, and I knew now I would not be taking this baby home with me. I felt comfortable in their company and appreciated how honest and open they were with their daughter about being adopted. They talked about fate and how it was meant to be. They were talking our language.

We exchanged numbers and told them we'd be in touch in a day or so. Even though I knew they were the ones, I wanted to talk to my dad and see if he saw anything of concern that I may have missed. Calling them with the news felt like an early Christmas present for all of us. There were four months left to go until they would meet their new child, and they kept in touch, checking in every two weeks to see how I was doing.

My sister and I took full advantage of our surroundings, spending time on the beach below the house, digging for clams while Erika played fetch with Duke. We took Erika scouring through the bush and discovered the remnants of a moonshine still. People lived in the woods all over the island, making moonshine and trading it with fishers for mussels and lobster. One early afternoon, we put Erika down for a nap and dragged Dad's boat out into the bay, tossed two fishing poles on the wooden floor and hopped in, hoping to catch something a few metres offshore.

We weren't going far, but Duke had a problem with our plan. He paced the shoreline, barking furiously, and after no response from us, he leaped in and swam toward us. The sun disappeared behind the clouds that blew in from nowhere, heading in our direction, and the wind became gusts, tossing our boat from side to side. Neither of us had life jackets; After all, we were only going out a few metres, we had thought. The waves took us further away from shore, and Duke tried to keep up. We dug deep with our paddles against the waves attempting to whisk us to sea.

Duke turned back to shore when we caught up and led the way to safety. We tied the boat and ran to the house to watch the full force of the storm enveloping the bay behind sheets of rain. We looked at each other, smiled, and agreed that Duke was much smarter than the two of us put together; He had known what was coming.

We didn't have money for Christmas gifts to send home to Mom and Grandma, so we made everything, including the cards and envelopes, but we had to have a Christmas tree, and the bush was the best source for the perfect tree. My sister spotted two trees, each having only one good side. With axe in hand, we chopped both down and wired the bad sides together to create our perfect tree, decorating it with homemade ornaments and popcorn garland. Christmas came and went with a heavy heart after talking with Mom; The tone in her voice cracked with the tears I envisioned rolling down her cheeks as we said goodbye.

It was 4:00 a.m. on February 2nd when I woke my sister and snuck into Dad's room to ask him to watch Erika and call Rudy and Janice; We were heading for the hospital.

Snowstorms on an Atlantic island are like no other area in the country. The snow is heavy, and the majority seemed to fall in February. It was still dark when we tossed my hospital bag in the back of the little Chevy, and my sister tucked herself behind the wheel while I breathed through each of my contractions in the passenger's seat. With every snowdrift we ploughed through, I'd scream. Each contraction hammered at my insides, and the two of us burst into laughter, appreciating our shared adventure. My sister was a skilled driver for her age and managed to maneuver between and around white mounds too much for the little car to take head-on.

Janice and Rudy arrived shortly after we were hustled into a room where my water broke, flooding the floor beneath my stretcher. Janice stood at my right side and my sister on my left, and I clenched their hands tight with the onset of the final contractions. My pelvis released the little body with a final push, and into the doctor's hands. A perfect baby girl took her first breath. I glanced down to see her for only a moment as they cleaned and wrapped her in a blanket and quickly whisked her off to the nursery. I had asked beforehand, when she arrived, not to lay her on my chest, as they always do with newborns. I squeezed Janice's hand and told her to go and meet her new daughter; She walked out and embraced Rudy outside my door. My sister asked me how I was feeling.

"Besides sore and tired, I feel good about my decision if that's what you mean."

My sister made it back to Dad's before the storm closed the roads all over the island, including those that were supposed to transport the baby to a different hospital. To make it easier for me, we felt the move was a good idea. In the evening, Janice came into my room to let me know they couldn't move the baby in the storm.

I smiled at Janice, and we held hands for a few minutes as I explained to her, "I'm good, Janice. More than good actually; I am great."

I knew I was making the right decision and have never wavered; This felt like it was meant to be in my heart and soul. She sat with me for hours; We talked about everything, and I shared my story. I asked for one thing from her: I wondered if I could give the baby a name. She agreed, and I gave her my mom's name, Rosemary. Janice suggested I write a letter or give her something to pass along to little Rosemary when she was older.

I asked my dad to bring paper and my pencils when he came to visit, and the next day, I presented Rudy and Janice with a drawing and poem entitled "Little Rosemary." The picture I gave her was the same compassionate face of Jesus, who sat on the fireplace mantle listening to my plea for help.

The thirty-day cooling-off period came, and I was happy to sign the final adoption papers; I knew Rudy and Janice were anxiously awaiting to hear whether I would change my mind. Soon after little Rosemary was born, my sister and I decided the island wasn't where we wanted to stay permanently, and she flew home ahead of me. I was booked to fly out after my appointment with Dr. Blackwood for my final checkup.

I was grateful to Dr. Blackwood for introducing me to Janice and Rudy, and I told him that I believed that divine help was no doubt a part of this beautiful story.

He took my breath away when he said, "Janice bonded so quickly with the baby that they are nursing."

I thought I had cried every tear inside of me, but this triggered an outburst of sobbing, and I asked, "How is that even possible?"

"Love, love!" was his answer.

Six months after Erika and I returned home, an anonymous note came in the mail; All it said was: *Little Rosemary is doing great!*

Every year on February 2nd, I light a birthday candle for little Rosemary, send out birthday wishes, and give thanks to the universe.

Dad was right when he said, "This is the beginning of your new life," as we stood on the deck of the ferry, gazing at the sunset.

That didn't mean it would be easy, because it wasn't. There were so many challenges and opportunities ahead, and I'd have to learn many of them the hard way, but I knew I had a calling to do something more, much more.

STARTING FROM SCRATCH AGAIN?

As a young girl, my dream of being an artist and designing furniture while living in a New York City studio apartment—complete with brick walls and oversized windows—was chosen based on something I saw or read. I didn't even know where New York was, but I was intrigued.

Our current circumstances, however, limited my choices. Art wouldn't pay our bills, and New York would have to wait. When Erika and I came home from our East Coast adventure, I had to find a job, a place to live, and we had to rebuild our lives. What little furniture we packed in the truck when we bolted to the island with my dad was left on the island, and we were starting from scratch.

I found a one-bedroom basement suite in a house within walking distance from my mom and stepfather, Don. It had a separate entrance from the main floor, it was clean, and I was elated to be one step closer to normal. I reluctantly applied for government assistance to get us on our feet. It was shameful for me to ask for assistance, whether it was government funding or help from Mom and Don, as not only did they pay for our flight, but they also supported us for the first two months of returning home to Edmonton.

Before we left the island, a friend of Dad's came by to see us off. He asked if I had any money to travel home. I had five dollars in my purse. He handed me a lottery ticket and said it was a winner, not much, but I could cash it in on the way to the airport. I added $86 to my fiver, and we got on the plane.

Government assistance gave us $550 to cover our rent and living expenses and another $350 to cover the security deposit for our apartment. Applying for assistance triggered the arm of the government responsible for collecting child support. I hadn't thought about child support from Erika's dad and wasn't keen on taking his money when he wasn't a part of our lives. The caseworker from Child Maintenance explained that the assistance program required support from the father. He was ordered to pay $150 each month, which we didn't receive directly until we no longer needed assistance from the program. When we started receiving the child support payment directly, I was thankful when the monthly cheque arrived, secretly sending out a wave of gratitude to the universe and Kelly. It wasn't much, but he honoured that monthly payment to the day Erika turned eighteen.

Finding childcare was the first task when I landed a position packing flower orders for a floral wholesale company. Mother's Day was coming up, and they were busy filling and shipping orders for retail florists across the province.

I was put in the receiving department and trained on the proper techniques for cutting and prepping the various flowers that came in. There was a chart on the wall naming each flower and all the greens, where they originated, and how to care for them. I unpacked and prepped tulips from Holland, roses from California and Equator, and I learned the differences between the rose varieties. Cleaning leaves off the rose stems under cool water and snapping the thorns that didn't stab me first wore my hands raw in my first week. I picked Erika up from Tricia-Glo Daycare and headed to Mom's in the evening. She smothered my hands in Vaseline and wrapped them in gauze which I wore to bed. My hands toughened up and became accustomed to the abuse in time.

I loved my job and saying goodbye to government assistance even more. I had always looked after myself, and after having watched Gina, who was more than capable of working, choose government assistance rather than getting a job, I was determined to be self-sufficient. I believed government support was a short-term solution for single mothers, and after seeing Gina and Maureen's family, I knew how easy it could be to get caught in the dependency trap.

I was, however, dependent on transportation. The logistics of getting Erika to daycare and then to work would have been two hours each way by bus, yet a fifteen-minute drive. I didn't have a car, and my only other option was carpooling. A gal who worked in the plant department upstairs offered to be my ride each day. I knew she had arrived at our place when we heard the heavy metal music thumping through the closed windows. On any given day, she smoked either cigarettes or marijuana before, during, and after work, drove like she stole the car, and each day, I'd say a little prayer as we made our way to daycare, to work, and then reversed the process after work. She was rough around the edges with a heart the size of the plant department, where she convinced the owner I should be transferred from fresh flowers to work with her in plants.

I knew the flowers inside and out, and had been working directly with retail clients in sales and support for the first half of the day. Then in the afternoon, I went upstairs to work in the plant department. The company owner had an office upstairs next to the plants. His son managed the flower department downstairs, and Mr. H., the old guy, had what looked more like a living room in his office. While trimming, watering, and packing plant orders, I'd hear the office door open with one of our retail customers emerging, straightening her hair, and giggling with Mr. H. as she descended the staircase to the front door.

It began slowly, with Mr. H. stopping to ask how I was doing and what I liked about my job. He'd inquire about Erika now and then, and when his chit chats became more frequent, he would get a little closer, to the point where I would see him coming from the corner of my eye; My heart rate would alert me, and I'd walk in the other direction. If he happened to walk behind me, he'd brush his hand across my back or my butt. This continued for weeks, and I dreaded my afternoon shift. He knew I needed the job. One afternoon as he walked by, he slid his hand around my chest and squeezed my breast before heading to his office. He'd called an afternoon staff meeting downstairs, where there were thirty people in attendance, and his son stood by his side as Mr. H. rambled on. My mind was on the incidents upstairs.

I was scared, angry, and I didn't hear anything he said until he asked, "Are there any questions?"

I broke the silence when I put my unsteady hand high in the air. He nodded.

I took a deep breath, and doing all I could to hold back the tears behind my quivering voice, I asked as loud as I could, "Because you pay me $6 an hour, does that give you the right to touch me whenever and wherever you like?"

There were gasps as people shuffled, turning around to see who posed the question. My knees shook, and tears welled in my eyes. I didn't prepare myself for this. *I might not have a job after this,* I thought. Was this a mistake? Mr. H. stared at me, his face crimson with anger.

He yelled back at me, "Yes, it does as a matter of fact, and if you have a million dollars to buy this company, you can tell me what to do!" He marched out of the room.

His son was soft-spoken, always friendly, loved by his customers, and when an employee had a problem, he was the one who would listen. He came up to me and hugged me as the room broke out in applause. He said it was courageous to say what I said and apologized for his father's behaviour. He assured me I would not lose my job and gave me the remainder of the day off with pay.

From that day, the atmosphere was different at work. Mr. H. never spoke to me again, and I worked full-time in the flower department again. The couch and other furnishings were removed from his upstairs office, signalling that my intuition was correct: When a female customer was behind on paying her account, he invited her to his office.

He, too, was a predator, and I had my share from the wolf in sheep's clothing, to the monster who was safely tucked away in prison, to the old pervert in the plant department. I thought for sure the golden gates of opportunity were going to swing wide open and invite me in. Had I not yet paid the price for the passage?

Not quite, bring on the con artists!

NOT AS IT SEEMED

I was happily working with the flowers again, out of Mr. H's reach in the greenhouse. After the famous staff meeting that everyone loved to talk about it, an opportunity came knocking, and I wasn't questioning whether it was a good move or not. Since it showed up, it must have been God at it again, making sure things didn't get too comfortable for me.

Pat was a regular floral customer, and I rushed into the cooler when she came in, eager to serve her and chat about her parrot who lived in her shop. She was a strong, confident woman, and I looked up to her as a role model. One day, she approached me and asked if I would manage one of her new stores. She and her husband, Gary, worked their anchor store in the famous Strathcona district, and I heard about the contract they landed with the fastest-growing grocery chain in the city. They were going places, so it was a big deal when she asked me to manage one of *HER* stores. Hello! Of course, I jumped at the opportunity.

Out of respect, she talked with my boss before asking me, and I was elated she picked me. I was top sales in the plant and fresh flower departments, and all the retail customers liked me. She assured me floral design training would be provided and what she wanted were my people skills.

I was moving up in the world; I would be a manager and didn't care that I had to take two long bus rides to get to my new shiny store.

We opened at the end of September, and my first task was to decorate for Christmas. After hours, Pat and her husband came in to hang new signage featuring a special on early wedding flower bookings. She taught me how to sell the brides and secure 50% deposits for their flowers and invitations. With Christmas arrangements, wedding bookings, and walk-in customers, I was run off my feet most days.

The everyday new stock would arrive. Poinsettias were everywhere, and I was determined to win the contest between the five shops—sell enough poinsettias, and win the Christmas cash bonus.

Once a week, a bylaw officer popped in and asked to see the business license.

He grew more agitated each time I shrugged and apologetically replied, "The owners are dropping it off. Soon."

The writing was on the wall, but I didn't read it. I was inexperienced, with no reference to why I wasn't receiving an entire paycheque every payday that came and went. When the boss came to drop off flowers and stock, he would hand me an envelope with $50 or $100 and assure me they were working on getting the payroll organized.

The poinsettias sold, and wedding bookings flooded in, with happy brides taking advantage of the winter sale. I locked the shop on Christmas Eve and went home with the envelope Gary gave me; This one had $200 cash, but still no real paycheque.

They will sort it out soon, I kept telling myself.

On Boxing Day, I made my way to the shop. As I approached the front door, a sudden and overwhelming sensation of dread washed over me. A sherriff's padlock held the chain securing the doors, and a note hung at eye level with bold black lettering: ***Permanently Closed.***

I stared at the sign and peered through the window at the empty shelves and remnants of cut flowers in the coolers.

Now what?

I used a phone in the grocery store to call Pat and Gary—no answer. I called the other stores. There was no answer at any of them. I dug in my purse for the home number of the manager who'd trained me.

She was upset and confused; The same thing happened to her and all the other managers when they'd arrived at their store that morning. We organized a collective visit to the accountant's office, which managed the company's affairs. We explained to the receptionist that none of us had been paid, and we refused to leave until we had answers and cheques in hand. After waiting a while, the accountant came out and told us there would be no pay for anyone; Pat and Gary closed all their shops overnight and left town. We talked amongst ourselves, firing questions at the accountant.

"But you're their accountant, can't you pay us? This must be illegal. How can they get away with this? None of us have our final pay or the Christmas bonuses we were promised."

His tone was apologetic. "It happens more often than you think. Yes, I am their accountant, but I can't do anything for you; I am only the messenger. Please don't shoot the messenger."

With that, he retreated to his office and closed the door.

We determined it was premeditated with the idea to sell as much as possible leading up to Christmas. The word was out on the street: They fled to the other side of the country, leaving behind a mountain of debt owed to all their suppliers. I was the only one who hadn't received a regular paycheque since I started.

I was young, naive, and hungry enough to take what they were willing to give me.

I thought about all those brides who trusted us with their wedding deposits, adding up to several thousand dollars between our stores. They were taken for a ride, and I was party to it. Thinking about how many people were hurt and used made me sick that someone could be so ruthless, dishonest, and uncompassionate. I was angry.

We had no choice but to let it go; We weren't getting paid and couldn't afford a lawyer. I had no money for rent, and daycare fees were due in a few days. I applied for employment insurance, but that would take several weeks to come in.

I had to make rent and pay daycare, and so I considered my skills outside of the floral industry. I had to do something to make money, but what? I sat down with pencil in hand and began to sketch. I drew old buildings that came to mind; They were always a favourite subject of my mom's. I sketched out a series of black and white images of decrepit old barns in wheat fields I had seen as a child. I looked at each one, adding a fenceline or post, or sprigs of grass in the foreground, and always a bird or two in flight off in the distance. When I brought them to where I felt they were ready to sell, I packaged them between sheets of onion skin paper so they wouldn't smudge and carefully slid them into a manila envelope. I took the bus to the floral wholesale to see my former boss, the good son. He was kind, supportive, and always cheerful. I knocked on his office door, and he gestured to come in and sit while finishing up a phone call.

I showed him the drawings I had and asked if he would like to buy them. He scanned each one, and we agreed on a price. We walked out of his office together, where one of his customers was waiting to have her flowers boxed up.

"We miss you here," she said to me.

I smiled and thanked her. He interrupted our chat to show her the drawings he had just bought from me. She nodded in approval and asked whether I would paint floral posters for her store; She preferred original art instead of the promotional posters from her distributors. I was elated that she saw potential in my art and she was willing to pay me for it. Two minutes prior to her request, I believed my former boss may have bought his collection as a pity purchase because he knew I was struggling.

Each morning, I took Erika to daycare, returning home to scan the newspaper for a job and work on the floral posters. I still needed a job; Painting flowers was fun, but I couldn't pay the bills doing that. Three days had passed when I locked-in on a job posting at a memorial company looking for an artist to design headstones. I figured if I could paint posters someone was willing to pay for, I could probably do art for headstones, so I applied and was hired on the spot.

This was intimidating and quite different from painting flowers. My job entailed drawing a library of illustrations for customers to select for their loved one's headstones. Every piece of art was hand-drawn on onion skin, flipped over and traced in reverse, and the graphite transferred to a sheet of mylar by rubbing the designs with a plastic scraper. The mylar had a self-adhesive backing, and once positioned on the stone, I peeled the support from the glue to secure the mylar in place. Once attached, I used a fine-tipped knife to prepare the face of the stone for the sandblaster. This cut required a steady hand with one fluid motion to follow the curves of the images and lettering. When I slipped with the knife, I had to start over, which happened a lot initially. The techniques I learned as a headstone artist proved to be valuable skills I've used ever since.

Mom and Don invited us for dinner often.

Each time we walked through the front door, Don would look at Erika and ask with a grin, "Are you at my house again?"

Our basement suite was within walking distance to both Mom and Don's and my new job. I didn't have to impose on someone to get us to the daycare and work every day. It was shaping up to be an unforgettable summer.

Mom worked full-time and often surprised Erika by picking her up after work and taking her back to her place, and I would meet them there for dinner. Erika often took it upon herself to invite us for dinner, something Mom never objected to.

On occasion, I would slow my pace walking toward Mom's house to catch a glimpse of her new neighbour. He had a beehive in the backyard, against the fence he shared with Mom and Don.

He often wore a t-shirt under his denim shirt tucked into his high-waisted jeans, and regardless of the temperature, he wore long sleeves. I noticed these details long before we ever spoke a word to each other. Still, when we finally introduced ourselves, I felt a familiar butterfly deep in my solar plexus that I hadn't felt since the day I met Kelly in the restaurant four years before. I didn't know whether it was Dave's New Zealand accent or the fact that he stood close to six feet and had dark, wavy hair and steel blue eyes. The whole package was quite attractive. He offered me a beer, and over Mom's fence, we chatted about the bees in his backyard. Apparently, we were short of beekeepers in Canada, and he was invited here as a beekeeper.

"Yay for the bees and me!" my inside voice was cheering.

Despite the closed door, squawking and chirping sounds could be heard in his house.

He glanced at the front window of his house and turned to me, smiling. "Billy and Rex," he explained. "I have a pair of cockatoos in the living room. I think they may be hungry. And I breed lovebirds upstairs."

He invited me to meet his flock, and I confessed my love for birds, telling him about our pet crow, Herbie Miller. My love for creatures wasn't reserved for birds either. I loved dogs of any breed, hamsters, rabbits, turtles, horses, pigs, goats, and cats too, even though I am allergic. Cats seem to know it and will do their best to tempt me into petting them, triggering an allergic reaction that sent me to the hospital on more than one occasion.

Dave and I dated long enough to learn that he wasn't for us, even though Erika and I moved into his house only months after we started dating. Having Mom and Don next door was great for Erika, and they loved having her visit every day after daycare. She helped Grandpa Don with his yard work and loved baking with Grandma. However, Dave and I grew further apart, and we argued about everything. His lovebirds lived upstairs in cages that stretched from floor to ceiling across three walls and had the the only heat register, leaving Erika's room cold in comparison. I kept her door open to draw in some of the heat, and fought with Dave constantly about prioritizing the birds over my daughter. It wasn't a difficult choice to get a new place for Erika and me. The idea to move was firmly cemented when my doctor told me I was pregnant, yet again.

Wow, I thought to myself. *How does this happen when I'm on the pill?* I knew I didn't want him in our lives; He wasn't the father figure I had hoped for Erika. The white picket fence I imagined at the beginning with Dave was a distant memory. Uncertainty and fear held me back from telling anyone about the pregnancy, and all I could focus on was leaving. As I had done before, I took inventory and began my plan. There wasn't a fibre in my body that rejected the idea of raising two children on my own. I felt ready, but was I?

I concluded this to be God at work, somewhat of an immaculate conception, and checked off the first item on my to-do list: therapy sessions. I wanted to either confirm what I was feeling or reach out for guidance. Maybe I was missing something. I felt grounded and confident that my feelings were correct; I was more than capable of raising two children on my own. My stepfather was concerned I may have contemplated abortion and was relieved to hear it couldn't have been further from my mind. I explained this to Mom and Don over a coffee date I invited them on to break the news. I told them I was as sure of this decision as the one I made to put little Rosemary up for adoption, and I was as excited as the day I learned I was pregnant with Erika. I believed it was God working the plan I wasn't privy to; All I could do, so I thought, was to trust the process and go with the flow.

I've known many couples whose marriages ended with child custody battles, alimony issues, and never-ending power struggles with the kids in the middle. Single parenting has many challenges, but I always considered myself fortunate that I never had to deal with the other parent, differences of opinions on raising children, or kids playing parents off each other. I had the floor, I made the rules, and though I made a ton of mistakes, I did it my way.

THE THREE MUSKETEERS

I had no intention of telling Dave I was pregnant because in my heart and mind, he was not father or husband material. He learned about it over a beer when my brother ran into him at a pub and spilled the beans, which made me angry at my brother. When Amy was born, Dave came by once to see her; She was a week old, sleeping in her reclining chair on the kitchen table.

His response was far from enthusiastic when he said, "So that's it, is it?"

I kicked him out, never to see him again.

I had found an affordable three-bedroom townhouse partially subsidized for low-income families. When Erika and I moved in, something told me I had better have our Christmas in order early, and sure enough, Amy was born a month premature—two weeks before Christmas. I felt like a nomad and had lost track of any treasured piece of furniture I may have owned along our journey. Did I give it all away? I always felt as though we were starting over. Some people have difficulties changing the style of underwear they buy or the paint colour on their walls, whereas I regularly changed more than the paint; The walls had to change too, along with the postal code. Everything seemed to be constantly shifting like a magnitude 4 earthquake. I learned to make decisions quickly and came to embrace change, to the point I would get bored and look forward to the next big thing.

The following summer, we packed again when the owner of our townhouse decided he was selling. Subsidized housing was a godsend for people like me. I was on employment insurance that paid a percentage of my wages. My $6 per hour salary wasn't sufficient to support the three of us, let alone the percentage I received. I decided to supplement my income by sketching black and white drawings of old buildings, as I had done before; I was sure I could do again. I drove to an upscale neighbourhood where mature trees cloaked streets that wound past the museum and overlooked the river. I liked bringing the girls to areas like this so we could soak in the scenery and dream of someday calling one of these magnificent properties our home. There were country homes I was especially fond of south of the city, and when the girls were older, we'd go for a drive, fixating on a few homes with fountains, ponds, horses, sheep, and goats, completing my dream of living in the country again.

I sat across the street from the houses I felt would make the perfect black and white sketch, and I drew them in detail. I took them home and finished the shading and final touches before returning to proudly knock on the doors of the houses I had sketched and try to sell them my art. I had two people slam the door in my face, and the third just shook their heads and closed the door. I couldn't believe it; Why wouldn't someone want a drawing of their own home? I felt deflated and broke. The drive alone was beyond my means—time to try something else.

Our new townhouse (number five) was too far to walk for groceries, Erika's school, and much too far to visit with Mom and Don. For unknown reasons, all available subsidized housing was in suburbia, where transportation was hit-and-miss with the bus system. When Grandpa Borg passed away, my brother ended up with his old Pontiac, a gas-guzzling monster of a car, which I drove sparingly. A full tank of fuel was outside my meagre budget.

My survival instincts kicked into high gear, and when I wasn't digging through the couch cushions for change to buy milk, I was scouring help wanted ads for a job that paid more than $6 per hour.

A friend introduced me to a printer throwing out a foil press that printed coloured foil lettering on stationery. It worked, and he said I could have it since he was replacing it with an automated version. He had several rolls of coloured foil that wouldn't fit his new machine. I took the lot off his hands and practiced in my basement with paper from Erika's craft supplies.

Uncle Norman, or, as mentioned before, we refer to him as Grandpa to the outside world, was a well-known commercial printer in Edmonton. I visited his print shop as often as I could, and I learned as much as I could absorb about the printing process. I loved it. I loved the smell of the ink, the paper, and the humming of the printing presses. I saw possibilities with the foil press gifted to me. I had an idea, and Uncle Norman (the industry leader) was the one to consult with.

My mother was always supportive of my dreams and ideas and clipped out an ad in the paper for a business program she thought might be of interest to me. A government-funded self-employment program was offered to anyone with a business start-up idea. I applied and was accepted to begin the program immediately. I knew it was a sign, another path presenting itself as part of my life plan.

Starting a business seemed like a manageable undertaking at the time. After all, I had the support of Uncle Norman, considered the last of his kind and held in high esteem by others in the print industry for his proofreading and typesetting skills. He was an old school master craftsman, and he sealed business deals on a handshake among his network of industry chums. I wanted to know as much as I could about printing, and he enjoyed having someone interested in his ancient printing process. I watched, asked a million questions, and learned only as much as he felt I needed. Though he was happy to share, he came from a world where women didn't belong in the industry; It was a man's trade.

He was a trade printer, providing commercial printers across the province with products only his machines could produce. I would stand clear of the heat radiating from the pot of lead he melted to cast his type, creating individual characters in various point sizes on his antique linotype machines, the only ones that were still in operation in Alberta, and maybe all of Canada, I was told. He would lay the type by hand, one character at a time, setting each letter upside and backwards to create perfectly aligned lines of text, and he proofread as he blocked the paragraphs to make the pages ready for the press. He was a master.

His passion for the written word, accuracy, and style was infectious. As I set the characters in place on my manual foil press, I followed the same technique as the pages handset by my grandfather, but on a much smaller scale. He printed beautiful tabloid-size pages, whereas I could cover nothing more significant than a business card.

I had a few friends and relatives who sold jewellery and makeup, and they paid me to produce their business cards. It was a tedious process, with one card at a time placed in the impression area; Then, with a button push, I stamped out each shiny business card.

I had high hopes and much ambition; *Amika Stationery* would undoubtedly become an empire.

THE ENTREPRENEURIAL SEED

When I started the self-employment program, Erika was four years old, and Amy was six months old, and the program schedule worked with the daycare hours. Starting a business at home would give me the freedom to schedule my time around the needs of the girls.

For a single mother of two, the prospects of getting a job that paid enough to cover expenses were slim. My old boss at the memorial company would have hired me back if I asked him, I was sure. Rolph was the owner, and he kept his sales manager through the winter, but since headstones couldn't be installed over winter, he laid off his other employees. When I worked there, it was perfect timing for a layoff when I learned I was pregnant with Amy. I thought about going back and asking him, but his sales manager and I were so misaligned when I worked there, and I didn't give it much mental energy. I understand sales can be difficult, and I can't imagine selling headstones to grieving families, but this sales manager took things far beyond my tolerance level; She didn't seem to have an ounce of empathy.

When I worked with her, I sat at the drawing table sketching out designs, a metre away from her desk. She opened the newspaper each morning to scour the obituaries. She'd grab the phone book and start her calls to the families of the deceased to sell them a headstone. I could hear the grieving family member on the other side of the call either scorning her for being so insensitive, or, so stricken with grief, agreeing to buy anything from her. I hated her approach to sales; She chased obituaries and preyed on people's emotions. As much as I loved to draw, I dreaded each day, having to sit and listen to her. I packed away the idea of returning to the life of a headstone designer in favour of exploring other ideas of what I could create and how I might venture out on my own with my foil press.

Fifteen people ranging in ages from thirty to sixty-five years young made up an eclectic mix of business ideas in the ten-week training program. Each week of interactive learning finished with a completed section of our business plans, and we were one step closer to launching our companies.

The first week began with self-exploration exercises about what I loved to do, my strengths and weaknesses, setting goals, and personal budgeting. The facilitator challenged us with "what if" scenarios that offered a wake-up call to those accustomed to earning a regular paycheque every two weeks. What if we didn't make any money? What would our contingency plans be? How much money do we want to take home? What is our big dream?

My business idea was simple. I was going to print business cards for every Fifth Avenue jewellery salesperson in the city, on my foil press and in my basement. My father came for a visit, and with his incredible skills as a machinist, he automated my foil press, giving me 300 imprints an hour instead of forty.

As we continued with the ten segments of writing our business plans, my struggle began when we took to the streets to determine whether there was a market for our product or service. I quickly learned that there weren't enough Fifth Avenue jewellery salespeople in the country to reach the revenue I wanted. Plus, I would need a team of people just like me, along with several foil presses to produce the volumes to earn the income I had dreamt about. I was at a crossroads to either change my direction and product or get a job.

The instructor explained that the secret to success at a start-up is to find a need in the market that no one else is satisfying. He encouraged me to go back to my market research and start again, which I did. While researching the outskirts of the printing industry, I went to the paper companies to see what they were doing and what was new or upcoming for paper products. The sales rep from one paper company showed me samples of two new papers made from recycled material. He explained that this would be the new kid on the block; No one was selling it yet. Bellbrook and Passport were the paper lines; They were expensive and not very attractive.

I took samples back to try on my foil press with little success. The fibres in the paper interfered with the heat, and the foil didn't take. I wasn't giving up; My intuition played a massive part as I continued my investigation to learn what printers were doing and the products they were offering. I met a couple of commercial printers who offered me a trade rate as a print broker. All I had to do was find customers interested in buying stationery printed on recycled paper.

I set out to learn all about the paper recycling process and how many trees were saved with every order of letterhead, business cards, or envelopes. I learned how the papers were made and discovered the bleaching process' negative impact on our environment. My goal was to become an expert in recycled paper, and I did.

I immediately revised my business concept, went into class, and presented my new business direction to my fellow students. Amika Stationery Services became the first company in the city to offer recycled paper products to businesses and "green" organizations. I completed my business plan and set out for a bank loan to fund my start-up and help purchase my $15,000 computer. The name Amika had a double meaning for me. Amy and Erika's names were combined, and I thought it was appropriate since Amika loosely translates as "friend" in many languages—the perfect name for my first business.

With my business plan complete, my stepfather Don accompanied me to the bank, and he introduced the loans manager to me. When we left the bank, I told Don that Wally reminded me of our librarian who was so generous with the strap. He laughed and assured me that Wally wouldn't be handing out any belts unless I didn't make my payments. He didn't admit it, but I was pretty sure Don and Wally had a backdoor agreement over my loan. Our facilitator told the class it might take a few attempts with different lenders to secure a loan; Mine seemed too easy.

Amika Stationery was born. Mom came to work with me part-time as an administrative manager, something every creative entrepreneur would benefit from. From day one, paperwork, bookkeeping, and any type of record-keeping went to Mom. We subleased office space from Abe, who repaired cars in the shop behind our office. He earned the title Bondo King because he didn't know what he was doing and used ten times the amount of Bondo necessary to fill rust holes. We were all learning our way to perfection.

When we were conducting marketing research in the business program, we had to conduct surveys, and insurance companies were on my list of one hundred calls I'd have to make. I called an insurance broker, and an agent by the name of Bruce picked up. When he heard the fear in my voice as I stumbled through the ten questions I had to ask, he laughed at me. Cold calling scared me to the point that perspiration ran down my wrist and dripped off the quivering phone receiver attached to my ear. My voice shook, and I froze during each call; I hated every minute of it.

Bruce suggested I come to his office so he could help me with my survey and delivery. He made a deal with me; If I bought insurance from him and sent clients his way, he would teach me how to cold call, and so I agreed. He came to our office every Friday afternoon. We'd pour him a coffee, and Mom usually had baked goods to share with any visitors. Bruce asked to see the list of ten calls I was committed to making every day, and we'd talk about closing sales; He made it all sound so easy. It wasn't easy, and I never learned to love cold calling.

Word travelled quickly about our line of recycled stationery, and the phone rang with orders from across the province. The media caught wind of what we were doing; The recycled "angle," as they called it, was newsworthy. We were interviewed and featured in Venture Magazine under *Tomorrow's Tycoons*. ITV interviewed and featured us on the six o'clock news, and a radio talk show invited me to share my knowledge about recycled paper and answer calls from listeners. I felt like a celebrity! Our business had taken off! And then it stopped. Like a tap turning off, overnight, the calls dried up; I'd call customers to learn they were buying their paper products from a big box store who was selling recycled paper below my cost.

I didn't anticipate this risk in my plan. *Tomorrow's Tycoons* became yesterday's story.

I couldn't compete, so I had to get creative—something I would later teach to other entrepreneurs. Creativity and a competitive mindset won't live in the same space, and competing with big box stores is futile; I had to make a change and fast.

The pivot was not easy. It wasn't an overnight smooth transition from our tiny office on printers' row to setting up at home in our townhouse. Cash flow slowed to a trickle, the bills were piling up, and Mom eased the burden by relinquishing her part-time office manager position with me.

She came in one morning and announced, "I really don't like paper, or the printing industry. I think I'm going to go back to the fabric store. They have a manager's position open." She asked me, "If you knew in the beginning how hard this was going to be, would you have started?"

Without hesitation, I said, "Yes!"

"Promise me," she continued, "if it gets too difficult, you will quit. Promise?"

"I promise, Mom."

And I meant it, but what I didn't know was *what was too difficult*? I didn't have any experience to measure difficult against since everything had always been a struggle. That was life, and I only saw the path in front of me.

Mom went back to the fabric store, and I set up my computer and equipment in our dining room. The girls weren't too happy about going to bed at 7:00 p.m. every night when their friends were outside playing, but this was my second shift. Days were reserved for sales and customer service, and I sat at my $15,000 computer at night. I was learning graphic design on the fly, and computer and software manuals were strewn everywhere, along with books on the best of graphic design I found at the library. I was learning the design program Corel Draw, and when a printing colleague commented on my style, I figured I must be getting good if I had a "style."

I drove a 1979 Toyota Celica, and when winter came, the heater quit working and the driver's door froze shut. It had a standard transmission, and I would climb over the stick shift to get in and out of the passenger door, and I'd bundle the girls up with blankets in the back seat. The temperature inside the car was as cold as the outside temperature, and the frost inside the windows was kept at a minimum with the cold air blowing from the broken heater fan.

Cash flow was tight, and I had to decide between house expenses or my business loan payment. If I defaulted, not only would I lose my computer and everything I worked for, but I also didn't want to disappoint my stepfather, or give Mom any reason to worry. I went to my grandfather, believing he would be happy to help since we were comrades in the printing industry. I asked him for a loan, and he asked me for collateral, which I had none, so the answer was no.

That was early spring. We had made it through the winter. I paid our bills and my loan on time each month, with barely anything extra left over. One day, I hopped in my car and drove out to the country to my secret hideaway, where I could clear my mind and hope the answers might reveal themselves. I parked along the edge of the creek and sat on the hood of my car, watching the water carve the remaining chunks of ice from the banks, reminding me this was a new season. I loved this spot as the only sounds were the birds, the water, and a distant hum of traffic.

I couldn't control the tears or the baseball-sized lump in my throat; I let it out, and my anguish burst into sobbing. I looked up and asked God to show me a sign, a path, or drop a bag of money on my head! Anything that would release the pressure. I asked, *What should I do?* My pride was bruised, I was exhausted, and when I couldn't cry another tear or think another thought, I said, "Thank you for listening," hopped back in my car and went to pick the girls up from school.

It worked out as it always did, and I knew that beyond a shadow of a doubt, we were always looked after. I didn't know the how, or what to do next except to pay attention. I knew we would be fine; I would land on my feet, and the three of us would be ok.

When Mom was back at the fabric store as a manager, she hired me to do odd jobs and paint indoor promotional signs, adding sign painting to my list of "I can do this," which became my mantra. When I was challenged with a design project for a furniture company, I said, "Yes, of course, I can do this." I became the queen of resourcefulness, and I rarely turned down a project. "I can do this," I repeatedly affirmed to myself after they asked if I could design their product catalogue and connect it with their inventory program, so it would adjust the inventory when clients placed their orders. My confident, "Yes, for sure, I can do this" quickly turned to, "OMG, I have no idea what to do first," so I hit the library.

There wasn't a Google back then spitting out answers to every problem known to humans. No internet, no email, and no easy way of transferring files between companies. I pulled every book in the library remotely related to what I was trying to do, drifting into computer programming, the driest subject on the planet for an artist. I needed to learn the program they were using and how it would communicate with the catalogue. I had never designed a catalogue either; I had a steep learning curve ahead.

Corel Draw wasn't intended for this type of work, but I managed to pull it off, all of it: the design and the connection. It was a clumsy connection, but it worked. I had software that spliced large files across several floppy disks destined for print, and I'd wrap an elastic band around the stack of disks and run them to the printer. Their pre-press people would open the files while I waited to ensure there wasn't a glitch, and if there was, I'd have to drive home and do it all over. This happened often.

The project was finally delivered, but they ignored me when it came time to pay their invoice. It was the only project I had that month, and I was relying on it to cover our expenses; I had a loan to pay, mouths to feed, and rent. I envisioned Wally at the bank, pulling the strap from his desk drawer. A daily visit to the customer's office turned up nothing except empty promises. Finally, on the fifth visit, I told them I would sit there until I had a cheque in my hand.

I wasn't one to share personal information with a customer, but this time, I scolded the sales manager who came from his office to deliver the bad news.

"They don't plan on paying you," he whispered. "You might as well stop coming by."

"How dare you! I did the work, exactly the way you wanted. I have bills to pay. I'm a single mom with two young children, and I'm not leaving here." By this time, I was sobbing.

He went into his office and returned with a cheque, his personal cheque, in the total amount of my invoice.

"I am sorry," he said genuinely, confessing, "This company seldom pays contractors like yourself, and you didn't hear that from me. Please take this." He placed the cheque in my hand and walked back to his office, wishing me the best of luck.

I didn't know who owned the furniture company until months later. I learned a prominent businessman who was in the courts, allegedly for tax evasion, owned the furniture company, and there was a list of suppliers suing him for non-payment. I thought about the sales manager who wrote me a cheque from his personal account and wondered if he too wasn't paid, recalling my time at the flower shop when I had a boss from hell. It happens more often than people realize.

I learned how to write up a contract and take deposits from that point forward.

AT THE ALTAR IN
A BLINDFOLD

My brother agreed to sell me his Volkswagen Jetta if I promised to get a few things taken care of, one of which was a significant dent on the trunk from backing into a garbage can. I took out a personal loan, which my new friend Wally at the bank was happy to help with. I don't know if Wally knew we were friends. The bank required me to also apply for a credit card. This would be my first.

My $5,000 loan got us a 1987 black four-door Jetta. Besides the block heater, there wasn't a single luxury option, and I didn't care; I was happy to have it. The interior was also black, and it didn't have air conditioning. In hot summer months, we relied on speed and green lights to keep us cool. The windows had roll-up style handles, and the power-assist steering was not as tricky as manual steering, but it was a bicep workout, nonetheless. I learned to drive a standard growing up, so I considered the five-speed stick a bonus. I loved that car. In our twelfth year, and three clutches and many memories later, the odometer turned over to 425,000 km.

Amika Graphics had enough work to keep the wolves at bay. I visited with clients and suppliers during the day when the girls were in school and daycare, and I'd do the design work at night after they went to bed.

On New Year's Eve, eight weeks after buying the Jetta, I had Amy in the passenger's seat on the way to the liquor store when we slid into the backend of a three-ton truck in front of the police station. Amy suffered a goose egg on her forehead when she hit the dash, at which point we learned airbags must have also been an option we didn't have.

The damage to the front of the Jetta was too extensive to drive, so I called a tow truck and had it taken to the nearest autobody shop while we took a taxi home. I followed up with the shop after New Year's. I walked into the service area to meet with the estimator assigned to my car. He stood to greet me, towering over me by two feet, thin and lanky, with dark curly hair and a welcoming smile. The brand of cigarettes on his desk matched the pack in my purse; He offered one to me, along with a coffee.

"What do you like in your coffee?"

"Nothing, thank you, just black."

He disappeared from his office as I leaned in to see my name printed on the top of the estimate he was working on.

"You spelled my name wrong; Most people do. Have you finished the estimate?"

"I have some bad news and some good news," he replied. "The car is a write-off, that's the bad news; But if you like, I can shop around for aftermarket parts and see if we can get the estimate down so the insurance will agree to fix it. Do you want us to write it off?"

"NO!" I gasped. "I just bought the car two months ago from my brother, and my loan is more than the estimate. I need my car. If you can find the parts, does that mean it can be fixed under insurance?"

"I'll see what I can do." Then he introduced himself. "My name is Orville, and here is my card. If you have any questions, don't hesitate to call."

He was smiling and offered to walk me out. I felt a pang of familiarity with him, a spark of chemistry between us. We both searched for things to talk about on the way to my rental car, walking at a snail's pace, prolonging my exit. He offered to fix the other items on my brother's list if they could salvage the car. He called each day to give me an update, with a side of small talk, and he was excited to share the news a week later—he found the aftermarket parts, and the insurance company accepted the new estimate.

"Come in to sign the paperwork, and we can get started."

He had a cup of coffee waiting for me when I arrived and moved his chair beside me to go through the estimate, item by item, detailing the origin of each part, and emphasizing how he built a relationship with his suppliers. They'd bend over backwards for him. He was digging deep for brownie points. I smirked at his overzealous effort with a job as small as mine since his regular clients were companies with fleets of vehicles. My car was fixed, and when I returned to pick it up, he didn't waste any time asking me out for coffee. We started dating.

Orville had a relative moving from a small town to Vancouver, and they had a dog they couldn't take with them. He asked if I knew someone interested in taking her, saying they would put her on a plane to her new home. I put my hand up without hesitation; It had been a long time since I had a pet. I'd had allergies to the cats we had growing up, and petting my rabbits for more than a minute sent me scrambling to the bathroom to wash before my eyes exploded into flaming red histamine reactors. Unfortunately, Amy inherited my pet allergies, but hers were magnified tenfold, triggering an asthma attack every time. Amy and I reacted to cats, gerbils, and rabbits, and we tried them all before this dog opportunity arose. We did have a short-term pet intake, a rabbit by the name of Sunshine, who should have been named Satan. He would hide behind the couch until I came into the room, and he'd attack my ankles with his razor-sharp Satan teeth. I tried to embrace the little monster and get in his good graces. Animals of all kinds love me, but not this guy. We took him to the animal shelter for re-adoption, and later learned he was a sweet loving critter after his new owners had him neutered. I didn't realize animal hormones are as volatile as PMS in women, though I've never bit anyone.

We eagerly stood outside the arrivals gate where special packages and crated animals were escorted from their flight. Admittedly, I was nervous; We had no idea what we were signing up for. The attendant opened the crate door and out stepped the sweetest, most gentle girl, a border collie by the name of Kelly. She smelled sweet, her long black and white fur coat was freshly groomed, and she seemed to smile up at me, her tail beating against the floor as the girls wrapped their arms around her neck.

She was five years old and eager to get outside, but not as enthusiastic about the car ride. The former owners told us she wasn't great with car rides or other dogs. She became the centre of our universe, with Erika taking on the role of caregiver and Amy dressing her up with clothes and accessories. She seemed to understand every word I said to her, and teaching her was easy. I'd tell her something once, and she'd obey—except when she was made to wear a leash, reducing her status from a human with four legs to a dog. She learned to walk next to me with one command, "Stay with mom," but she much better without the leash and proved to be the star when the afternoon bell rang at school. I took her with me every day to pick up the girls, and Kelly lit up when kids poured through the doors and beelined toward us. She loved the attention, and her herding instinct wasn't wasted, bumping each of the kids to move them into place, or laying low and staring down her opponent when she saw another dog approach.

I am sure the only reason I met Orville was to meet our precious Kelly dog. When I reflected on our relationship, it was difficult to pinpoint why else. Once again, I didn't explore qualities foundational to a healthy relationship, and once again, God was the scapegoat in the end. The girls and I had lived at the townhouse for five years when Kelly joined my little family. I had dated Orville for almost a year when my landlord announced the upcoming sale of our place, and over a coffee, Orville told me of a rental house he'd found. Without any discussion of children, finances, future, values, dreams, the strained relationships with his own kids, or anything else that may have slapped me upside the head with a stop sign, we decided to rent the house together. My white picket fence syndrome overshadowed any logic. I was lonely and always wanted a "family unit" and a father figure for the girls. I got a father figure all right, the familiar figure I grew up with: my dad.

We moved to the house and got married in the backyard, much to the dismay of Erika. My brother gave a speech at our wedding which included saying, "One thing I can say I love about my sister is she sees only the best in people." What he really meant was that her new husband is a loser, and God bless her heart for taking him in.

Orville lost his job shortly after we were married, and I became the sole earner with expenses four times what I was responsible for in our townhouse. I couldn't keep up with the bills and sent my resume to an employment agency. They sent me to a temporary graphic design position with a technology company that owned five subsidiary businesses. It was located in a rural town, forty-five minutes from the house, and I would be earning $12 an hour.

Orville told me he didn't drink when we met—one of the things I liked about him—but he was drunk every day once we were married. He managed to get a truck driving job but needed a credit card for purchases on the road. He had no credit, no bank account, and I obviously had no brains. I gave him my Visa card.

Working outside of the house and driving an hour and a half each day kept me hopping and focused on myself, the girls, and our schedules. With my new position, I didn't have the time or the energy to keep up with Orville, and I chose the ostrich survival strategy to keep the balls in the air—with my head buried deep in the sand. I think my subconscious knew what was going on, but it didn't come to the forefront until the day I came home early from work. SURPRISE!

Orville was standing at the kitchen sink with his usually groomed curly black hair tussled, his half-buttoned shirt hanging outside of his jeans, and there was a pretty petite blonde sitting at my kitchen table who looked like she ate my cockatiel, Moe. I looked over at Moe's cage in the corner, and she was still inside with the door closed—something we never did when we were home; She had rein of the house.

Orville introduced her as a co-worker; She too drove a truck. *Well, isn't that special*, I thought to myself. My head was spinning. I didn't know what to do, or to say. When she left, Orville cracked another beer and retreated to the living room without a word.

I sat at the kitchen table with our stack of bills and opened my credit card statement. There was a list of $50 cash advances withdrawn at a truck stop Orville frequently ate at when he was on the road.

When I asked about the charges, his response was usually "Don't you trust me?"

I wanted to because it was easier than knowing the truth, and I scrambled to pay off the balance each month since cash advances warranted a higher interest rate.

I pulled my head out of the sand when I learned there were prostitutes, known as lot lizards, that hung out at the truck stop, and they charged $50 for their services. I quickly called my sister because she had taken a trip with Orville several months before. Maybe she could dispel my theory, but she only confirmed it when she told me that he had tried to get her in his sleeper. Through my sobs, she tried to explain that she wanted to protect me and didn't think telling me was in anyone's best interests.

When he came home that day, I was in the garage painting a landscape I titled "After the Storm." When he walked in, I confronted him about my sister, the $50 charges on my card, and the little blonde I met in my kitchen the day I came home early.

He stared back at me and without any emotion or even a glimmer of remorse, he asked, "When do you want me to leave?"

"Right now."

I turned my back to him and gently swirled the paintbrush on my palette as my knees grew weak. I held my tears until I saw him drive away. I sat in front of my canvas and cried like a baby.

Everyone around me seemed to feel I needed to be sheltered from the truth. Even Erika, who was elated when he left. She revealed how horrible he was to her when I wasn't around, continuously putting her down and calling her names. *WTF? How could I be so blind?*

Amy had a different relationship with him, and they got along quite well, yet she brushed off her disappointment rather quickly when she found out he was gone. *I've failed miserably as a mother,* I thought. My intention was to build that white picket fence fairy-tale family unit, and at that point, I had to pack away my feelings and make some tough decisions.

I set up an art studio in the basement of that house, and to supplement my income—now that I was a single parent again—I taught art classes to kids in the neighbourhood on weekends. Within three months, another surprise landed at my doorstep: The owner of the house gave me notice that he was selling, and we had to move. My graphic design job that began as a ninety-day contract had grown to six months, and I approached my boss and asked to make it permanent. They bought out my contract with the agency and increased my pay to $18 per hour.

A friend invited me to a real estate seminar hosted by a mortgage broker presenting a sure way to buy a house without a large down payment. I learned that if I had an RRSP (Registered Retirement Savings Plan), which I did, I could borrow against it. I didn't want to get my hopes up, but maybe, just maybe, I could finally buy a house of my own. The process took longer than expected, and we had to make a short-term move to another townhouse I found for low-income families. We stayed there through the winter while the broker worked his magic, and to my elation, it worked. I bought my first home on my own, using the little I had tucked away in my RRSP. The lawyer wasn't too happy when I told him I was in divorce proceedings, so I had to get Orville to relinquish any rights to my new house before the sale went through.

I worked with a team designing tradeshow booths, brochures, logos, and anything that could be printed. At first, I was intimidated by the high-end, up-to-date equipment and software, the best on the market. My supervisor handed me the keys to a world I had never known. My little company may have produced graphics for customers, but nothing to the level of what I was learning in my new position. We designed and printed most of our materials in-house with our state-of-the-art large format printer. When I started my first business, in-house colour printing was out of reach. The first desktop colour printer I saw at a tradeshow used a coloured wax technology, and cost $30,000.

Our large format system used the new four-colour ink sprayed onto the surface of the coated paper through forty-eight-inch lines that travelled back and forth with the print head. Considered a workhorse in the industry, the printer worked best when it was in constant production. When days would lapse between large print jobs, one, two, or all four colours of ink would stop flowing and ruin the project, sometimes inches from completing a ten-foot banner. This happened often and seemed to rear its ugly head when the deadline was the following morning. Erika was sixteen and had always been a responsible teenager, so I was comfortable leaving her home with a friend on nights I went back to work to finish my projects, while Amy slept on a blanket under my desk.

When we outsourced printing, I was given the green light to bring in printers I had been working with for years. I spent time in the studio of the photographer we hired for product shots, and our department was given the job to plan and create our Christmas party, with instructions from the boss to stay within our $30,000 party budget.

I watched and learned as each of the five subsidiary businesses rolled out new ideas and products. One company, or division as I called it, built a plant south of the city to produce a pipe coating that reduces the build-up that causes corrosion in pipes at high heat levels, and our product was expected to revolutionize the industry. The coinage division produced coin blanks for the federal government, the chemicals division produced water treatment products and our medical division was led by a scientist who invented a silver-coated dressing for burn victims. And finally, the flat-screen technology division which was up against well-known names like Sony, in a race to reach the market first.

The atmosphere in the company was electric, and our graphics department was on steroids, trying to keep up with the presentations, events, and marketing material for the five divisions.

I loved my job, but one day, we learned our supervisor was being investigated for theft, and his computer was seized. I was one of three who remained in the department, and each of us was interviewed by human resources and the company lawyer. Apparently, our supervisor was staying after hours and printing projects on our equipment and selling them to his outside clients. After a twelve-year career with the company, he was fired, triggering a chain reaction of layoffs and department changes. I was then tasked with creating a budget for the department and a two-tiered billing system: one tier for design and one for production. Anyone ordering from the graphics department would have to fill out a job requisition with a job number assigned to each project.

The writing was on the wall. The pipe coating division was in trouble. They sold the coinage division, and hundreds of people working the assembly line in coinage were laid off. Our TV technology division had a succession of problems from the start. Our department had created all the branding, produced presentation folders, brochures, business cards, tradeshow displays, printed shirts and hats, and shipped everything to a technology show in the US. I got a call; They had to change the division's name and everything we just produced. No one bothered to do a name search beforehand, and the name they chose was already in use by another company. Not one out of the many lawyers in the legal department that stretched across the entire second floor did what every new company does—a name search.

I watched and listened as company budgets were cut, including the upcoming Christmas party. This time, there wouldn't be trips to anywhere Air Canada flew as one of the door prizes, like the year before.

My boss was the manager of HR, and she called me into her office to let me know our department was considered non-essential and would be closing on October 31st, one month from the day she handed me my pink slip. I knew it was coming and had the letter ready to send to everyone I had worked with during my time with the company. I went back to my office, revised the letter with the date of our department closure and sent the email, announcing I would be offering graphic design through my own company as of November 1st. The hammer of her heels against the tile floor grew louder as she walked the hall leading to our department. She was mad.

"Shauna, you shouldn't have sent that letter."

"Why not? Everyone knows we are closing the department. What are you going to do, fire me?"

We laughed together, and she offered me a bonus if I stayed to help dismantle the department, sell the equipment, and deliver files to each of our internal clients.

They gave me a deep discount to purchase the computer I had been using. I was grateful since I had to sell my system at home to pay for the lot lizards Orville charged to my credit card. He may have been out of the picture, but I was still cleaning up from that relationship.

They paid me a generous severance when I left, and I relaunched my company as Madsen Studios. My former internal clients followed me. My career always seemed to land on solid ground, but my relationships with men always seemed to end in the middle of a minefield. My intention was good, but my selection was not. I often wondered whether I was fooling myself by justifying my choices by claiming God's will was behind everything. I deeply regretted the negative impact my relationship with Orville had on the girls, especially Erika. There was always collateral damage with a boatload of guilt that sailed alongside me.

No matter which way I looked at it, I couldn't let go of the idea that I was meant to meet Orville. I would not have bought that house or taken that job, changing the direction and quality of the work I was doing, and in the end, positively impacting both of my girls. I went from a $6 an hour wage as a waitress and a high school dropout to managing a graphics department for a high-tech company, and I never lied on my resume. I chalked it up to God having a hand in everything. I didn't realize I had been in survival mode for so long, and I didn't know how else to respond to life but to put it on the Big Guy upstairs. Besides, it was all meant to be, according to the code I shared with my dad.

When she was in her early teens, Erika asked whether she could meet her dad, and I said I'd give his number to her if she still felt the same way when she turned sixteen years old. On her sixteenth birthday, she asked again. I pulled the phone book out, knowing he would be easy to find since he hated change, and I figured he would be close by. She sat with a friend and called Kelly, and they booked a day to meet for coffee. I asked to talk with him before she hung up, and I told him he had to meet with me first.

He and I met at a restaurant where sixteen years of pent-up anger was discharged across the table at warp speed, and I left nothing out.

When I was finished, I asked, "Why didn't you come and rescue us?"

He shook his head, "I don't know."

I wasn't expecting an answer; In my heart, I wanted him to know how difficult the past sixteen years had been, and I wanted to beat him up a little, or a lot, and I suppose I needed to vent in a big way. The truth was, I didn't see how life could have unfolded in any other way. If I had married him, little Rosemary would not have been born to that family, and I wouldn't have Amy in my life. It was unthinkable.

I told him that if he wanted Erika in his life, he would have to step up and help with her post-secondary education, and he agreed. They met and began what would become a beautiful relationship, and it could only have played out the way it has. When I heard about Kelly's strict house rules from his family and his stepchildren, it confirmed in my mind that we were never meant to raise Erika together, as we would have strangled each other.

ANOTHER DETOUR
IN THE ROAD

The shiny new house I was so proud to have bought on my own needed a lot of work, especially in the yard. I worked nights and weekends, adding flower beds and weeping tile to stop the water that ran down the hill from the house and flooded the floor in my one-car garage. I dug out the garbage and rocks from the vegetable garden buried there by former renters. I planted shrubs, hedges, and laid a stone pad for my barbecue alongside the stone patio I stained to look like slate.

I worked in the sun and the rain, and almost daily, my new neighbour, Denise, would either lean on the fence to visit while I worked, or she'd join me on my two-seater patio set my mom and Don gave me for a housewarming gift. Denise and I would have coffee, and she'd sneak a cigarette now and again while we talked about life, marriage, raising children, and anything in-between. We watched the sun go down over the neighbour's roof before calling it a night. Denise became a lifelong friend. I adore her for her candor and sense of humour, and I respect her for the work she did for so many years as a caregiver to her elderly clients.

Denise had been living in her house for thirty years; She had divorced several years prior and had one grown child who became a teacher. Her story was encouraging; I wanted both my girls to leave me in the dust when it came to their education. I reluctantly told her that I only completed Grade 9, with a few extras I had under my belt from Loser High.

I was proud to share with her that while I was pregnant with Amy, I learned I could challenge the Grade 12 level exam without taking any of the prerequisite courses. English was my favourite, outside of art, so I challenged the test, earning my credits for Grades 10, 11, and 12. Sometimes, I took classes or workshops related to my work. By this point in my life, the idea of getting my high school diploma didn't appeal to me in the least. Instead, I went to university for art classes and later received top marks in business communications and project management, neither of which required a high school diploma.

Making it to where I had without a diploma didn't mean I wasn't eager to see my girls reach their full potential. My dad's words were burned into my memory, when he pulled me from Grade 10 and said that school wasn't for me. I vowed to encourage my girls to stretch and work hard, and yes, stay in school. Life is much easier with education than without.

While Erika attended university, she worked in a restaurant, earning enough tips to buy her first car. She learned to drive a standard in the Jetta by sitting in the passenger seat with her hand on mine, listening to the engine and watching the odometer, and she'd shift as I pushed and released the clutch.

The day I asked her to do my grocery shopping, I tossed her the keys as she skipped to the door, announcing, "I feel like an adult."

My sister insisted I put an ad in the paper to meet someone, and if I didn't, she would put one in for me. Kim scoured the ads until she found one and relentlessly pushed me to respond to it until I finally conceded, writing a letter to the man who said he had a sense of humour—and he wasn't hard on the eyes.

I met Nick at a restaurant, and when he walked in, I wondered if he rode a Harley motorcycle since he had a full tawny-coloured beard that merged with his sideburns, framing the dimples and accompanying his pleasant smile and shoulder-length wavy hair. *If he has a bike,* I thought, *at least he is somewhat of a handsome biker.* When I asked, he said he used to ride. He then told me he had met another lady in the same restaurant the day before, and I was a breath of fresh air. I supposed he was shopping for a lady friend. He wasn't the type I usually found attractive, but he was interesting, and I agreed to meet him again. When he introduced me to Pink Floyd, he asked if I had lived under a rock all my life. We played cribbage, backgammon, and darts. We laughed together, read *The Hobbit* together, and took trips to the mountains every few months. We were having fun, more fun than I'd had with a man, perhaps in my whole life.

Nick had a house on the northside, and we made the big decision to move in together. Neither of us wanted to live in the other's house, so we sold both of our houses, bought one together, and married in 2003.

My mother said to me, "I've heard about this before, but I've never seen it until now; He changed the minute you two were married."

I am a very positive person, the sunny side of life has kept me moving forwards, so it shocked my system and everyone else when I married again; But this time, he made Oscar the Grouch sound like Betty White.

I'm glad she could see it because I thought I was losing my mind when he became an angry old man in what seemed like an overnight transformation. Everything we had done together before ended abruptly. He sat at the table after work waiting for his dinner to be served. What I had done before, just to be nice, he now expected, like getting up at 5:00 a.m. to make his lunch. And now he complained if I put too many or too few carrots in his lunch box. It had to be ten olives and no more. OMG, how to sweat the small stuff. When I took a stand and told Nick he could make his own lunches, he was furious.

A year into the marriage, I began secretly seeing a therapist in hopes to work through relationship issues, primarily the relationship I had with myself. Marrying for the third time should have been different, better, and forever.

Nick was mean to Amy, and she was never one to endure bullying from anyone. When she was in kindergarten, she chased a Grade 6 boy through the playground and pulled his pants down in front of his friends in retaliation for teasing her.

Getting back at Nick, she laced his sandwiches with stones or worse; She scavenged the backyard for evidence the dog was there and scooped some as a condiment for Nick's food. They were like water and oil, and as much as I tried as a referee, nothing made things better at home. He believed children should be seen and not heard, and I was childish because I did everything I could to have fun (and poke the bear), like starting a food fight with Amy by flicking a pea at her from the tip of my spoon. Peas were flying, we were laughing, and Nick was not. He pounded his fist on the table, called us names, and marched to the bedroom, slamming the door behind him. We laughed some more. He exploded when she took the phone out of the kitchen, and little by little, everything either one of us did, he jumped on.

I was still doing graphic design from home and thought hard about getting an office, a place outside to call my own space. That would be the first step. I wanted out. I needed my freedom again.

One afternoon after visiting a client, I passed a retail store I had driven by a thousand times and didn't notice before. The

FOR-RENT sign in the window tripped me, and my car turned a sharp right into the small parking lot. An elderly gentleman in coveralls stood on a ladder working on the eavestroughs. I walked over, introduced myself and asked about the space. He said it was his son's place and passed me a note with a phone number. I hadn't considered a retail location; I was thinking more along the lines of an office, but I thanked the Big Guy upstairs. If it was meant to be, it would all work out.

I called the minute I walked in the house, and he said a few people were ahead of me, but they only wanted half the space.

I told him, "You want an art gallery there; It would be perfect for the area."

I was willing to take all 1,200 square feet, so he wouldn't have to put up any walls. The gallery idea came to me as it spilled from my mouth; I had not put an ounce of thought into it, but now, game on. He said the space would be available in six weeks, and I signed the lease without hesitation.

I shocked myself. *Shauna, what are you doing?* I shook my head. *Well*, I responded, *I said an art gallery, which is what we will do. I can do this!* The next six weeks were a blur. I wrote a business plan to include the art gallery, picture framing, and flowers. I chose picture framing since every other gallery I visited offered the service, and having a flower cooler I thought was wise as a way to attract people who may otherwise be too intimidated to enter a gallery. Besides, I missed working with flowers and always wanted a flower shop to call my own.

Applying for a loan took longer than expected, so I dipped into the small nest egg I kept from the severance package from my former job. I planned on continuing the graphics, but the business license was strictly for retail so that any business support in the way of graphic design would be done quietly or reserved for artists who needed help with marketing.

A graphic client introduced me to an art dealer, Roger, who had a substantial collection of art stored around the city in warehouses—works of art from his former days in his gallery, most of which were paintings from the 1970s. I knew little about his artist's pieces, except that he didn't look after them, and many were damaged and needed new frames.

My mom was thrilled at the opportunity to work together again, this time, surrounded by art, and she committed to part-time hours. We taped paper on all the windows as we worked inside, cleaning and painting and setting up counters. I found a small used floral cooler at an antique store north of the city. I was looking into the prospects of renting art to customers, and Roger liked the idea. We agreed to sell and rent his art, filling the walls with works by Austrian painters, koi fish art by renowned watercolour artist Joseph Raffael, and early works by local celebrity artist Alex Janvier. Dozens of artists' work covered our walls.

We were so green initially. We had no idea who the artists were, and we didn't know how to frame pictures. We started taking a crash course in both. Our frame supplier sent over Doug, their salesperson, and he gave us the basics of what we needed for frame moulding samples. He clued us in on upcoming trends, and he helped us with a pricing schedule. He didn't expect to be paid for his knowledge, so Mom had homemade cookies for him when he dropped in. He showed us how to use the tools, measure, and price each project using united inches, linear inches, and square feet, and what each type of measurement was best suited for. I was delighted to learn that the framing industry used the imperial system and not metric. The printing and graphics industry also used imperial, so I was one step closer to catching on to our new trade.

We found a used front door from a former Booster Juice store. We hung it early in the renovations, and the buzz in the area was not positive. People were not happy about a retail chain moving into the neighbourhood.

We pulled the Booster Juice label off the front door to get ready for the Madsen Studios sign I spent a month of evenings building. My former sign-making experience came in handy: I cut the letters with my jigsaw, added texture in plaster, and finished it with a patina finish. We hung our new eight-foot sign above the former Booster Juice door and had custom canopies made and installed over the windows. The landlord found a vintage outdoor light, which completed the curb appeal.

We were open for business, with a few flowers in the cooler. We advertised fresh bouquets on the six-foot Inukshuk sign I cut from plywood and painted in terracotta red, orange, and mustard yellow; He stood proud on the sidewalk, screwed to a stand I found in the basement.

Even though we opened the doors as a soft launch, our first framing customer walked through the door on day two. We measured up their artwork and chose the matting and frame as Doug, our favourite person in the world, showed us. A second and third framing customer walked in, and we repeated the process. We learned our roles quickly; I was good at the design, and Mom loved the assembly. But we had to get the pricing thing down first. I reviewed the quotes we gave our first few customers, and something wasn't right. The first one was more than five hundred dollars; The others seemed very high too, so we called Doug. He laughed, explaining we had our square feet and linear inches mixed up. I called each customer, and they were delighted to learn I made a mistake in their favour, and the price was a quarter of what I had told them. They became raving fans and sent their friends and family to us for any framing. The Booster Juice door proved to be an unplanned marketing strategy, with people popping in to talk and thank us for not opening a retail chain, and they too came back as customers.

The Highlands neighbourhood was home to a few art enthusiasts, far more knowledgeable about what we had hanging on the walls than we were. I made it clear I was not an expert, though I loved art. They would educate me on a few pieces and the artists behind the work. I had no problem telling people what I didn't know.

Several of Roger's pieces needed to be fixed. This gave us hands-on experience in the framing department.

After picking up supplies, I returned to the shop and said to Mom, "Cathy at the frame supplier told me she is a certified professional picture framer. We are posers, Mom."

She laughed. "Maybe we are, but we don't hide the fact we are new to this, and we are doing a great job as posers."

Roger's work was selling, and we reframed several, recouping our costs when the art sold. This infuriated Roger; He didn't think we could sell his work and said he thought we would rent more instead. The collectors in the area told us the actual value of a few pieces they bought from us and let us know they got them for a song. I suggested that Roger review his prices; He was leaving money on the table.

We were getting ready for a grand opening. Erika worked on our marketing plan as a project in her university program. She already had her journalist diploma and was working toward her marketing degree.

Roger marched through the front door a week before our big event and announced, "If you don't make me a partner in this business, I am taking all my art out. You have forty-eight hours to respond."

We stood, stunned by what just happened, and watched as he slid into his rusty Mercedes with bald tires.

Mom and I looked at each other, and I said, "No fucking way anyone is going to threaten us or give an ultimatum. Not a chance."

I picked up the phone. Six months before the gallery idea had landed, I had been sitting at my kitchen table with an art publisher who presented a magazine filled with artists, and I had happened to know two of the artists he was featuring. He'd sold me a full page to feature my art for $1,500, payment upfront. Full payment should have been a red flag, but it wasn't, and he'd disappeared with my money. I contacted the artists in the magazine he'd left behind, and they told me their stories. Each artist had given him money and received nothing in return. One woman said she'd handed over her life savings and was so distraught that she quit painting, and her cancer returned.

I called a meeting with the artists—there were twelve of us—and I listened to their stories. I told them I contacted every art gallery in the province to warn them about the publisher and explained that there was little we could do legally after I talked with a lawyer.

"But what we can do," I suggested, "is turn this into something positive and form an art group, work together, and support each other."

And that's what we did.

These were the artists I called that day Roger threatened us. We offered the artists space to show their work and agreed on a commission split. I told them of our upcoming grand opening, and they were delighted to bring their pieces in. Mom and I took all of Roger's paintings off the walls, wrapped them in brown paper and put them outside, and I called him to let him know he'd better come and get them before it rained.

PETS ARE THERAPISTS

A lifetime of therapy sessions was spared, and hundreds of thousands of dollars were saved by the unconditional love from every pet I've ever had, except for the psychotic rabbit, Sunshine.

It is my experience that every animal (a cat, bird, dog, rodent, or turtle) has a soul, a unique personality, and a purpose. I've never understood the sport of hunting, and burned into my memory is the movie *Powder*, the story of a boy who is connected to life in such a way that he is sensitive to the feelings of every living thing. The scene that moved me to the core was when the young boy came across hunters, and one hunter had shot a deer that hadn't yet died. The boy grabbed the arm of the hunter and reached for the deer with his other hand. As the deer fought for its life, gasping for air, the boy held tight to both, connecting the two and forcing the hunter to feel what the deer was feeling. That scene portrayed the connection we have with all things living.

I've held many of my pets as they passed on. I've always known when it was time to say goodbye because they decided for themselves, and in their way of communicating, they made it clear that they were finished on this plane.

While I was still with Nick, my beloved dog Kelly passed away. Erika and Amy grew up with her, and she was only five when she joined our family. I called the vet first, and then Erika. She was living with a friend, and though I couldn't bring myself to say the words, I strongly suggested she come by that day to see Kelly. We all knew it was time. She was seventeen years old and could no longer walk or get up from her bed on her own. It never gets easier with the passing of a pet, no matter how many times we have to say goodbye to yet another one. Amy came with us, and the two of us were inconsolable for days. As days turned into a month and then two, the void that Kelly left was glaring, and I decided to fill it when I walked into a pet store for one of my regular bird visits to see if there was anything new.

My love for birds never waned from the time we were kids and my brothers brought home Herbie Miller, our pet crow. In the pet store, they had a young parrot, Cooper, who walked onto my finger without hesitation, and it was love at first sight. This little black-headed caique was a clown and loved to cuddle. SOLD. I gazed into Cooper's eyes while the cashier rang in the cage, all the accessories, and Cooper, for a cool investment of more than $3,500. I didn't blink. I didn't care how much he was; He was coming home with me, and I forgot to consider Nick. Oops. This is the kind of decision most people make as a family.

I bought a second cage for our store and took Cooper to work every day, no matter the weather.

I'd open my jacket and say, "Get in."

He'd hop in, nestle in my neck, and stay there until he knew we were inside. I took him shopping, camping, and on trips to Home Depot; He'd poke his head out of my jacket to see where we were and climb up onto my head when he knew I couldn't grab him while I cut wood at the self-serve saw.

On my trip to the lawyer's office to go over my divorce papers, I learned quickly how many people fear birds. Cooper came with me, and several employees hid behind their desks when I walked by on our way to the boardroom. As the lawyer and I talked, Cooper hopped across the boardroom table from one end to the other, picking up pens and chewing on sticky note pads along the way.

If I left his cage door open at the store, he'd sit on top and wait for Mom to walk by. If she wasn't paying attention, he'd lunge at her. One afternoon when I was designing a flower arrangement, Mom shrieked and came running to the back with Cooper hanging tight to the skin between her thumb and index finger. She feared him, and he was jealous of anyone close to me—they had better be on guard. It's common for parrots to choose one person as their favourite, but Cooper loved Amy too, likely because she wasn't scared of him.

Cooper was four years old when he developed a lump on his back that grew by the day, and the vet concluded it was cancer and removed it. She warned me that it was the type of cancer that could return, and six months later, it happened. I placed Cooper in the kitchen window on the perch I made him out of a tree branch, where he finished his morning rituals with a small piece of peanut butter toast. After he was done, his leg kept slipping off the branch, he was shaking his head, and I thought he was going to fall, so I picked him up. When he climbed on my finger, he moved slowly and seemed to lose his strength by the minute. Over the next two hours, his little body trembled in my hands. He made sounds I'd never heard before and began flailing his wings uncontrollably. I knew his cancer had returned, and I knew by how rapidly his symptoms were progressing by the minute that this was our last day together. I held him tight to my chest, sobbing, telling him how much I loved him, and thanking him for being the most incredible little buddy I could ever have been blessed with.

As his actions became more violent, I knew I had to do something; I couldn't allow him to suffer another minute. I took him into the bathroom and ran water in the bathtub, intending to submerge him and put him out of his misery. I cupped Cooper in my hands and knelt in front of the tub.

I held him tight, kissed his little belly, and sobbed.

"I'm so sorry. I don't know if I can do this. Oh my God, I can't let you suffer, but I don't know if I can do this."

With that, Copper calmed down completely, leaned in and took my thumb in his beak. He squeezed firmly as his eyes faded to grey, and his body relaxed into weightlessness. He left before I had to do the unthinkable.

I was told by the vet that people who love birds develop a relationship with their avian pets with a bond much like a human relationship. I know it. That day my heart broke in pieces, and I mourned the loss of Cooper as if he was a best friend, which he was.

Soon after Cooper's passing, I took my first holiday out of the country, tagging along with my siblings and their spouses to Mexico. Before I left, I found a house and began the process of purchasing, which is a much bigger ordeal when you're self-employed. My mom managed the store while we were gone, and I gave her the task of finishing the house purchase if it unfolded with the bank while we were gone.

I was standing in the town square at an outdoor market in Sayulita, Mexico when Mom called. We completed the purchase over the phone with the bank, and I returned from holidays as a new homeowner. We called it the Hobbit Hut: a two-bedroom, 480 square foot bungalow with a single garage and within walking distance from the store. I put in a new kitchen and bathroom, and changed the flooring, only hiring a professional, when necessary, as I did much of the work myself.

I quit smoking on October 20th, 2007, shortly after my divorce with Nick was final. I was living intentionally and shedding unhealthy relationships and habits—therapy sessions taught me that the relationships I've had throughout my life were habitual. These habits were brought forward from childhood, with scars from the trauma that I had never dealt with. I didn't know I had anything to deal with, believing it was all just a series of events and circumstances that were meant to be.

Three months after I bought the Hobbit Hut, I found Gracie online. She was a rescue dog from Mexico, apparently, a mixture of Beagle and Dachshund, brought to Canada and put up for adoption through an animal rescue in Edmonton. She was living with a foster mom, eager to introduce us after I completed the screening process. Normally, they have a meet and greet session and give the potential new owners time to think about it. The minute I walked up to the door and my eyes met with Gracie's, I knew. The connection was instant, just as it had been with Cooper. I didn't need to think about it, so I signed the papers, paid the fees, and took her home the same day. She was a senior and lived out the remainder of her life in comfort.

I believe rescue animals are grateful and understand they were chosen. After Gracie's passing, another introduction online resulted in two miniature dachshunds, Reba and Rocky, siblings, and again, seniors in need of a loving home.

They are our best friends and companions who love us unconditionally, and all they want in return is the same.

THE PRIEST, THE ART, AND THE CLEANSING

The shop was like a sanctuary to me. I loved interviewing artists who brought their work, hoping we'd select theirs to be included with the other artists. I rarely said no, recalling how intimidating and deflating it was to go through the submission process with a "real" gallery, only to be rejected. We weren't going to put the artists through that, and the only submission process we had was to have them come in with their work so we could chat. I loved to learn about the art, the artists, and the stories behind their work. When I shared the backstory with a customer contemplating a piece, the backstory closed the deal.

We had a mix of paintings, photography, glasswork, stone carvings, pictures of all descriptions, ironworks from a local blacksmith, and pottery by a master potter who lived in the area. My mom took watercolour classes from one of our featured artists, Willie Wong. The day she came to work and saw the blank space on the wall where her poppies hung the day before, she stood a little taller and cried when I told her it had sold. We featured over fifty-five artists during the four and a half years we were there.

Erika arranged a framing deal with a chain of restaurants, and Mom was kept busy assembling orders. In addition, our

135

flowers were a huge draw. The floral design skills from my time when Erika was three hadn't been lost; I was better than before. As a part of Erika's marketing program, she put together a plan for a Garden Art Show, an event we hosted on the last weekend of May each year before the summer festivals began and filled every summer weekend in Edmonton. Our glass artist, Patricia Doyle, joined us from Vernon, BC with her tools and demonstrated lampworking techniques, and painters created alongside each other under the twenty-four-foot tent erected in the yard. Our flower supplier gifted us 200 roses for the first people attending, and they were gone in two hours. Adding a barbeque was a great way to support a local charity, with their team of volunteers flipping burgers and hotdogs.

On this day, we gave the artists 100% of their sales rather than splitting the commissions, and even though the shop earned very little revenue during the event, we drew crowds, and our client base grew year after year.

Father Thomas worked at the church two blocks from the shop. When he heard we supported local artists, he introduced himself as an amateur photographer, shooting God's creations as he called his body of work. At six feet and four inches, he towered over me, and he glowed in his serenity, making a statement with his presence before saying a word.

In his early thirties, with sandy blond hair he wore a little longer than other priests I've met, Father Thomas was eager to display his work in our shop. We helped him with his pricing and framing, and it didn't take long before he and I became fast friends, spending hours walking along the river talking about God, one of my favourite subjects since I was still on my spiritual quest, and he had so many answers.

I asked how he became a priest.

"I was called by God to this work when I was in a rock band. I woke up one day when we were on tour, and the message could not have been more straightforward."

God told him that his calling was spiritual, and we talked a lot about God, spirituality, and religion.

One afternoon, he happened to be driving by and saw me sitting in deep thought at the picnic table in our yard. My wandering thoughts snapped back to the moment when I heard the gravel shift under his tires as he rolled up in his sedan. He seemed to fold himself in half getting out from behind the wheel, stretching his long leg from the open door, dipping his chest into his knee and pushing his torso up and out, followed by his other leg. *Driving must have been uncomfortable*, I thought to myself as he closed the door and came to sit on the other side of the table, facing me.

He seemed to sense I needed to talk. "What's up?" he asked.

"I've been having nightmares the past few days and disturbing ones, and I haven't had nightmares since I was a young girl."

He asked what I'd been working on recently, and I told him about a customer's three-panel artwork that was initially smuggled from Cambodia; The panels had scratches across the face of all three, and I explained that I went to her house a few times and spent several hours trying to fix the damage. I described the artwork was a triptych, each panel measuring four feet by two feet and too heavy to transport, the reason why I went to her home rather than bringing them into the shop. There was one image across the three panels of warrior women fighting from the backs of elephants. It was composed in black ink and mother-of-pearl, with a thick resin poured to seal the image to the back, giving it a gloss finish, except for the scratches I was trying to fix.

I sheepishly asked Father Thomas, "Do you believe that the energy of bad experiences from the past can hang on to objects?"

And I was shocked by his answer.

"Absolutely" was his response.

He explained he had studied a variety of religions, beliefs, and cultures, and he was well-read on topics such as energy, the law of attraction, mindfulness, and so on. He told me everything is energy, and energy cannot be destroyed. If the artists were under duress while creating the art, one might be picking up on that. Energy can stay with objects and people.

Having studied a little about energy myself, I agreed with him, but I told him this was different.

"There is a feeling of evil in my dreams, not of stress, or oppression or anything like that."

He asked, "Would your customer agree to have her home cleansed?"

I paused for a moment, thinking about the woman and the stories she told me of her daughter who had died, and how they'd had regular conversations beyond the grave. Her daughter had wrote her own eulogy for her funeral. Apparently, she'd wrote it after she died. The woman performed all types of incantations and rituals, calling on the dead to bring her daughter forward. She freaked me out with her stories, but my curiosity always got the best of me, and I listened.

I responded, "Yes, I think she'll be all over this idea; She's into all types of metaphysical stuff."

When I called her, she jumped at the chance to have a priest in her house.

"This is exciting. See you next week," she said in closing.

I pulled up to her home to meet Father Thomas; I waved as he pulled up beside me. I was a little shocked to see what he was wearing as he stepped from his car. His never-ending legs poked through the bottom of his long dark coat, buttoned to his neck. He leaned into the passenger's seat to retrieve a black case.

"Wow, Father, you look a little familiar," I said, remarking on his outfit and how it resembled the priest in the scariest movie ever written.

It's only the most frightening for me because I have never seen another horror movie after my brothers made me sit through the original film of *The Exorcist*.

I asked, "Is this going to be an exorcism?"

"No," he responded. "It's quite a few steps from that. Consider this as more of a cleansing."

Once inside, and the introductions being complete, Father Thomas opened his case and reached in to pull out a white cloth, gently draping it over his left arm, followed by a white bowl and a small bottle that resembled an antique perfume decanter. Next, he brought out an aspergillum, used in ceremonies to sprinkle holy water, and finally, his Bible.

"You will assist me."

He looked in my eyes as he placed the bowl in my outstretched palms. He poured a shallow pool of holy water into the bowl while whispering a prayer of gratitude.

"We will start in here," he instructed as we stood in the doorway of the den.

Father Thomas blessed each corner of every room and finished in the living room, where the triptych took up a large portion of the feature wall. He sprinkled holy water around the room while reading from the Bible, and with every cast of his wrist, he would cleanse the space with gratitude, prayer, and scripture.

As he finished, he turned to my customer to explain what just took place.

I gasped, "LOOK, LOOK!" I hollered. "Look at the artwork."

They spun around to witness all three panels glowing from the backside, and through the art, radiating and shedding light on every detail. The mother-of-pearl glistened, and the warrior's expressions appeared to have changed from fearful to joyful. The three of us stood together in silence.

I worked on those three pieces for hours. The images were dull. The design lacked depth, and there wasn't anything remarkable about the art, except for the detail and how the artist painstakingly laid tiny slices of mother-of-pearl to create these intricate images. That impressed me as an artist, but there had been no emotional connection until now.

While Father Thomas turned to my customer, I stayed put, staring, absorbing the experience and the divine results we witnessed together. There was no doubt in my mind that this was divinity in action.

Father Thomas spoke to my customer in a stern tone. He instructed her to refrain from reaching out to people who had passed; He warned that she had no idea what she was working with and that it was dangerous.

We talked outside for a few minutes before heading back to our everyday lives.

"Did that just happen, Father?" I asked, already doubting myself and my eyes.

"Yes, it was quite remarkable, wasn't it?" He continued, "While talking with her, I sensed that she likely won't stop what they are doing, and she will open that door again. It's a door to a dimension she knows nothing about, and it can be hazardous. All we can do is show them the way; If they choose another path, we can do little to stop it. That is what free will is all about."

He slid into the driver's seat and set his bag of cleansing tools on the passenger's seat.

"Thank you, Father Thomas. I am deeply honoured to have been a part of this incredible experience with you."

Several years after we sold the shop, I reached out to Father Thomas to ask him for a specific photograph of his, one he took while still at the church down the street. The church wanted him to lead a parish in Scotland, where he and his wife started a family.

He responded to my request with a phone call.

"I wanted to talk to you directly and not through email," he started. "Of course, you can use any photo of mine, but I want you to know how you and your mother impacted my life. You were so supportive and always encouraging me to pursue my photography, so much so that the church sent me to a photography school, and I am taking photos of God's creations everywhere."

I was shocked and honoured to have been a part of Father Thomas's artistic career, and his outpouring of gratitude made me see a quality I hadn't noticed in myself. Supporting others in following their dreams and passions seemed like a natural response, and I had been unaware it was a strength of mine and would be an asset in my next career adventure. I was gathering stones of knowledge on every path I chose and was pleasantly surprised with the fork in the road that was quickly coming into view.

The landlord was raising our rent when Mom had decided it was time to retire. She was sixty-nine years old and had spent the better part of her working life in a retail career, making her the best merchandiser for our shop. I told her I didn't want to do this without her. The timing seemed fitting since the lease was up for renewal; I decided we would wrap things up before another Garden Art Show. After telling a customer about our plans to close, he brought a friend in who asked if she could buy the business, and she did.

The sale was an asset sale, since she couldn't buy the name Madsen Studios, and the actual value was in our systems, supplier relationships, and our extensive customer list. I offered to take her to each of the suppliers, introduce her, and go through the customer list with the information we had, what they preferred for flowers, who was a repeat frame customer, etc. Mom had a book she started on the first day of business where she tracked the daily sales, the weather, unsold roses, and arrangements after Valentine's Day and Mother's Day. It was brilliant and worth its weight in gold. The new owner didn't want any of it—the training, the introductions, or Mom's daily diary. She took the customer list, floral supplies, and some packaging, and seemed more interested in the wine cooler we had in the back.

I lost sleep for months after selling the business to her, dreaming I was inside the shop after hours and making flower arrangements for the regulars that came in. I wanted to look after them. My dreams of breaking in and invading her place continued for nine months.

In the final episode, she caught me, red-handed and said, "What are you doing in here?"

Putting the final touches on a flower bouquet for a regular customer, I barked back, "I'm looking after the customers because you're not."

And with that, I woke up.

I learned the following week that she closed her doors. My dreams of loitering her shop ended the same week.

NEW KEYS
OPEN NEW DOORS

Erika told me that her dad's wife had left him, sending a shock wave through our family and his. Kelly hadn't told anyone about the separation and carried on with his acreage life as he always had, working long days as a truck driver before heading home to an empty house, where the trusty can of stew awaited and he'd watch TV until it was time for bed. It broke Erika's heart to watch her dad living his life on autopilot. Erika is a problem solver extraordinaire and concluded all she had to do was find a good woman for her dad, and while she was at it, her mom deserved to have a good man. She invited the two of us to events and dinners as a group. She didn't know how to respond when I told her that her dad had come into the shop and asked me on a date.

Kelly and I dated for nine months before I moved from the Hobbit Hut to the acreage. The spark we shared when we met in 1981 hadn't dimmed in the slightest, and it grew brighter as he revealed the side of his personality I fell in love with so long ago. A kind and gentle soul with a quick wit and genuine interest in listening to others—really listening. Likely the most reliable man I had ever known besides my stepfather, Kelly was always there to lend a hand, and he did what he said he would do. He has always had a reputation in the trucking industry for his passion for maintaining the truck and equipment he was responsible for, and his acreage reflected the same attention to detail. Three acres of rolling hills with the greenest grass in the county, and to my surprise, only two miles from the area the girls and I chose for our weekend country drives years before.

The white rancher with attached double garage and wrap-around verandah had been Kelly's home for twenty-five years. He cleared trees at the back of the property and built a 1,600 square foot shop with a mezzanine and in-floor heating—a man-cave fit for a king.

Once I was settled on the acreage, Mom moved into the Hobbit Hut, a short drive to the Holyrood long-term care residence where Don would live out the remainder of his years after the doctors said he could no longer live at home. Mom was also caring for her mother as Don's condition deteriorated, and Grandma had been living at the Holyrood home for five years. This was Mom's first choice for Don's final home, but there was a waiting list.

The staff loved my mom, and she was always eager to help, whether it was mealtime to help feed residents or with weekly laundry, often taking resident's torn clothing home to mend. I was astonished at the condition of some of the clothes piled high on her table.

"Don't the families buy their parent's clothing?" I'd ask Mom, holding the threadbare undershirts to the light. "You could spit through this."

"It's sad," she replied. "Too many residents have garbage for clothing. I suppose the families think, why bother spending the money? They don't go anywhere, and then some haven't visited since the day they dropped their parent at the front door, so we keep mending the same clothes."

When the call came that Grandma had died, my brother and I met Mom at the residence to say goodbye and pack Grandma's belongings. The staff kept her neatly tucked in her bed for our final visit and tidied her nightgown and hair before we arrived. We looked at each other with a grin. They had put her teeth back in her slender mouth, and they stood proud behind her paper-thin lips, too large for her hollow cheeks.

My brother broke the silence. "They don't quite fit anymore, do they?"

We snickered and hugged Grandma, agreeing she was still beautiful; She had the smoothest skin, and there were barely any wrinkles on her ninety-six-year-old face.

We packed up two small boxes of photos, knick-knacks, and a silk flower arrangement I'd made when she first moved in here.

I'd reminded her during each visit, "These are silk, Grandma, so you don't have to water them."

And each visit, I took them into the bathroom to drain the water in the sink.

With Grandma's passing, the residence had a vacant bed, and rather than opening it up for someone they didn't know, they offered it to Don. One week after Grandma passed, Don was moved from the hospital to the residence. Once he was settled, like clockwork, Mom visited every other day and booked the small guest dining room for dinner on Thursdays. Each week, she asked Don what he would like; She cooked his favourites, packing it in her insulated bag, adding his favourite relish or pickles and dessert she'd made that day. This was their weekly date night. With each passing year, we celebrated his birthdays in the atrium, and Mom picked him up for family dinners, wrestling his wheelchair in the back of her car and maneuvering him into his chair when they arrived.

Parkinson's robbed him of his ability to smile, weakened his voice to a whisper, and reignited his childhood stutter. He never complained. I looked into his eyes on one of my visits and told him a joke.

It took great effort to respond through his stuttering whisper. Apologetically, he said, "I'm sorry, I can't laugh at jokes anymore."

"It's ok, Don, you're smiling with your eyes."

I fought back the tears until I left and lost it on the way home; I had a conversation with myself and God. "It's just not fair." I thought of all the times he's been there for my sister and me. He lost so much in his life and never felt sorry for himself. His only daughter passed away when she was three years old. His son Gary died of a drug overdose, another son, Keith, died from AIDS, and a third son was homeless, by choice, for as long as we' had Don in our lives. His remaining two sons and their families spent little time with Don; We were much closer to him—one of us visited him weekly. Don would never gossip and always pointed out the positive side of a negative situation. "He is a good man," I agreed with myself. I love my father in the east but acknowledged to myself in the car on the drive home how grateful I was to have had Don in my life. I may have a father, but Don was my dad and a glowing example of human kindness.

Don passed away on July 12th, 2018, at eighty-four. Mom stayed in the Hobbit Hut. Before she moved in, there were a few things I wanted to do to the place for Mom's comfort and safety. The sidewalk blocks were dangerously uneven and deteriorating, so we had a new sidewalk installed over the old with a unique rubber paving product. Mom had never had a garage to park her car, and I wanted that for her. According to the garage door estimator, the single car garage could have used a can of gas and a match when he came out to measure for a new overhead door. I had asked if he could install a new overhead door with a remote door opener.

"It's like putting lipstick on a pig, but we can do it."

"Hey, it's my pig, and I want a door."

I completed several renovations before moving to the acreage, including flooring, a new kitchen, a new roof on both the house and garage, and I painted the stucco and the trim on both buildings. The overhead door with a remote opener was for Mom, but what she did for the place turned the Hobbit Hut into the talk of the neighbourhood. Mom has a natural gift for landscape design, and combined with her green thumb and gardening knowledge, she could transform any yard into a gardener's oasis, and that is what she did.

We had a forty-foot tree in the front yard, with four trunks baring branches that stretched to the neighbours on either side, gifting them with leaves to be bagged by the dozens each fall. They hated the tree and asked me to cut it down every year. When Mom moved in, we had an arborist examine the split between the trunks; It was rotting, so the neighbours would be granted their wish. It took a crew of five men over three days to cut the tree and haul it away, giving Mom a blank canvas to create her gardens the way she saw fit.

After five years of designing, nurturing, and a whole lot of love invested in the new yard—a landscape only Mom could create—she won first place in the Tiny Yards category for the contest the city runs every year. Each year, she competed with herself to improve and add more ideas; The lawn served as a frame for the flower beds and greenery tiered by colour and size, each variety blooming at the perfect time as though they passed a baton between them. The Yards in Bloom first place award is proudly perched front and centre, where passersby congratulate her and thank her for contributing such beauty to the neighbourhood.

PIVOT IS
MY MIDDLE NAME

When the dust settled with the shop's sale and it was time for a new adventure, I visited an old friend. David finished his call and motioned for me to come in. He leaned back in his chair, clasping his hands behind his head, and smiling.

In his thick British accent, he asked, "How are you doing, Shauna?" (Sounding more like "Shorna.") "How is the retail business?"

"I sold the shop," I responded. "Mom wanted to retire, and I wasn't interested in running the shop on my own or hiring anyone; The lease was up, and it was a good time for a change."

"Come work for me; You know our program. Besides, I just got a new government contract to work with childcare operators to improve their business skills, and you'd be a great coach."

David was a shining example of entrepreneurship. He'd left engineering to pursue his dream to develop programs and teach. He was brilliant, enthusiastic, and with a "call it like it is" mentor style. I went through his program years before to fine-tune my graphic design business plan and discovered a passion for planning.

David's company was a community partner with a federally funded program, providing microloans to people under thirty-nine years old with a business idea and a plan, then called the Canadian Youth Business Foundation, and rebranded years later. David was one of the first community partners. He invited me to join the loan review committee to review applicants' plans and mentor them through the loan process.

He wrote the childcare program, and his team delivered it to childcare centres in need of business support across the province. I had the northern region, visiting centres in remote areas, advising and coaching the managers and directors to develop their plans, help with marketing, and get a snapshot of their financial situation. It was clear they started their childcare business for the love of children; They were stellar when working with the kids. The business side, however, was difficult and frustrating, and they knew they needed help.

A few months into my contract, David called me to meet and told me he had terminal throat cancer. He let me cry my ugly cry, passing me the box of tissues, and when there was a break between sobs, he assured me that he'd made his peace with dying. I asked him if there was anything he wanted to do, any bucket list items.

He shook his head. "I hate travelling, and I've been everywhere I've ever wanted to go. I honestly have no regrets and no unfinished business. I'm good."

Such an awkward moment—what was I supposed to say to that? I wanted to fix something, do anything, but he insisted he was good. I hugged him and went home. He passed away within two weeks of our talk.

He completed the sale of his business shortly before he died, and I approached the new owner and asked if I could move from childcare into the classroom as a facilitator. She needed one, and I wanted to learn how to teach. For the next eighteen months,

I facilitated ten-week classes, back-to-back, with up to sixteen students in each, ranging in ages from twenty years to sixty years.

David had developed an intake process, and when I wasn't on the road heading to a childcare centre, I had helped David with the applications for the self-employment program I was now teaching. He had simple requirements for applicants: They had to have a viable business idea and the means to fund their start-up. If they didn't have the cash, they needed access to funds through good credit to apply for a loan or have an investor in the wings. David insisted on quality candidates because they had a better chance of success. As a result of his criteria, the program had a high success rate of start-up businesses at the end of the program.

The criteria disappeared with the new owners. We joked that the requirements had changed; They were accepted if they were breathing. With each group of students, the quality of applicants deteriorated. During our assessment interview, I turned away one applicant only to find her sitting in my class on the first day. She went to the owner and complained, and the owner told her she was accepted. I wasn't enjoying my time there anymore, and the owner and I butted heads on any idea I brought to the table.

Bums in seats equalled revenue; No students meant no income. During my final class, a student asked to leave early to take her four children to the dentist while still having coverage through our program.

"I don't know what you mean," I questioned. "This program gives you dental coverage?"

"100% coverage," she replied.

I was taken aback and had no idea that fourteen out of sixteen people sitting in front of me had benefits paid for by the program I was teaching.

"You've got to be joking" was my reaction to the hands in the air when I asked the class who else had benefits. "Do you realize I am a self-employed contractor here? I am in business. I am where you want to be; There are no benefits from the government to cover dental or prescriptions and whatever else you get. I am self-insured with everything. I pay for all of it. That's what businesspeople do, for God's sake."

With that, I marched into the owner's office and told her how appalled I was that those students were here for the benefits. I told her there wasn't a hope in hell that most of them would ever start a business. Half of them couldn't put two sentences together. One student planned to open a restaurant, but he had no money, no car, and the bank denied his application for a personal bank account. Yet, while in the program, he was encouraged to finish and present his plan to a bank.

"You are setting him up for failure," I told them. "Even if he had great credit, there isn't a bank in town that would finance an unproven restaurant, and you know that."

I finished the program with the class and wished them all the best. The new owner and I argued when I told her I would be hosting planning and marketing workshops for existing small businesses. She was angry. I gave her the idea before and suggested we could do it together. Instead of having government assistant students, we could teach existing business owners who can afford the training. Maybe they could use a refresher and a new perspective on their business. I also suggested we take the program online, and she scoffed at that too.

I moved on, focused on my own business, and launched a series of workshops on planning and marketing. I was always hungry to learn new skills, and so I enrolled in university level courses specific to my needs. I wasn't working on a degree like the students half my age sitting beside me. I wanted knowledge I could apply. Since

I was designing magazines, coordinating articles, photography, page structure and deadlines, project management seemed like a good fit. When I managed the graphics department for the tech company, I took computer courses, creative writing, and writing for business. I've always been an avid reader, and my bookshelves have always been stocked with what my mom calls "that self-help stuff." She prefers murder mysteries, determined to become a forensic investigator in her next life. My collection is made up of spiritual and business treasures, blending ancient wisdom with new age insights on personal growth and business development.

I didn't say no to many projects; Dad's code still whispered in my ear as opportunities presented themselves. It must be for me, or it wouldn't have shown up. And they certainly showed up, from every direction. I worked seven days a week, twelve hours a day, reacting to clients' demands and agreeing to every deadline and request; I felt like I was on a fast-moving train, with no off switch.

There was little joy in my work, and I had become a puppet to a couple of clients, at their beck and call at any hour of the day or evening. My sister brought me into a land development project she was working on with a national home builder. They hired me for the branding of a development in the Okanagan, a reprieve from the demands of my other clients. I became a marketing and sales team member, leading the creative process and brainstorming sessions. I loved the work, and when the VP of Marketing told me I'd make a great marketing manager and offered me the position, I took it.

I wrapped things up for my business, finished projects with a deadline, introduced another designer to the clients in need of long-term attention and flew to Toronto to begin my new position as national marketing manager. Our team would be responsible for implementing marketing strategies for the residential properties, resorts, and marinas they owned from coast to coast. Until I arrived at head office, I didn't know I was trading one bucket of stress for another.

Our team worked remotely, with weekly meetings over conference calls, and in the first month, we set goals for ourselves and our team. Rheagan was the marketing coordinator for the western provinces; We worked together on the Okanagan project before I became an employee. She flew to my region from Vancouver to plan and host grand openings, and together, we'd visit properties across the province. On one of our road trips, we had to find a place to park the car so that I could call in for our weekly marketing meeting. Our boss was the vice president of marketing, sales, and home construction. On our calls, he asked for updates from each of the managers, and he always saved my report for last.

In his stern, unwelcoming tone, he asked, "What's going on with marketing?"

Before I gave him my report, I liked to start each call with something light or fun and perhaps unconsciously to poke the bear; My introductions were something our boss hated. I imagined him rolling his eyes or turning shades of crimson since he always seemed angry with me. I'd begin with a story or anecdote to soften the tone and wake up anyone that might be snoring on the call.

"Well," I began, "Rheagan flew in from Vancouver, and we are on a road trip, heading to Pine Lake for a site visit. We had to pull the car over for this meeting with you today, so welcome to southern Alberta. Picture this if you will."

The other people on the call were silent, and Rheagan sat in the passenger's seat, grinning with anticipation.

I continued, "We pulled over, onto a side road, the sun is shining, there is a slight breeze, and a bright yellow canola field is to our right. While each of you shared your reports, a field full of cows started to make their way toward us, and right now, as we speak, there are a dozen cows lined up, side by side, staring at us. Did you know that cows are inquisitive?"

Rheagan was laughing, and we could hear laughter echoing in the background through my car's speaker. Our boss did not laugh; He was angry, as usual, and told me to forget the stories and get to the marketing report to tell us what's going on.

I was not cut out to work in a corporate environment, far too structured, and too many rules that made little sense to me. It took less than two years for me to realize their values and mine were not aligned on any level. I loved my work and my team, but the stress of butting heads with my boss wore me down.

The degree of my stress wasn't evident until I left my position. They had me sign a non-compete agreement when I started, and I was bound to that agreement for six months after I left. I went to my doctor, who sanctioned days each week for mental health appointments in addition to his regular practice. I unloaded my mental baggage on his desk, and he put me on stress leave.

When I returned to the entrepreneurial world, clients were happy to have me back, and I resumed a couple of contracts, but something was different. The spark that once lit my path wasn't quite as bright. I went through the motions, returning to what I thought I should be doing with branding, marketing, and business plans. I knew the work; it was my comfort zone until it wasn't. I felt empty, and Kelly and I were struggling with our relationship; I was shocked at how much-unresolved resentment I had toward him. Though my head convinced me and covered the grief by telling me it was meant to be, my heart still ached over Kelly's response when I told him I was pregnant over 30 years ago.

There were more than 200 people at the women's conference, and I sat at a table in front of the stage with seven others, listening to the speakers, one by one, talk on their topic of expertise. The final presenter of the morning was Coach Stacey, a popular speaker, admired by many as the life coach who walks her talk, and she exuded confidence and warmth as she took the stage. She talked about longings and discontents, addressed the critical areas of our lives, and asked us to do an exercise.

"I'll give you two minutes to rate how satisfied you are with each area of your life, from one to ten. One is not satisfied at all, whereas ten means you are very satisfied."

I hid my answers from the others at the table; I knew this exercise would reveal how bankrupt I felt in all areas. 1. My Creative Expression, essentially my work, I was generous with a FOUR; 2. Spirituality, I felt disconnected, though at that moment I decided that God probably put me in that chair, so I wasn't going to beat up on my relationship with God, so I gave myself a THREE; 3. Relationships, only thinking of my marriage, since my other relationships weren't causing me discontent or longings to speak of, so I gave it a TWO; 4. Health, I lumped my physical, mental, and emotional health for a total of THREE; and finally, 4. Money and Time Freedom, I didn't have any sense of freedom and saw this category as sister to the first category, and since I hadn't reached my financial goals, I felt a TWO was an honest assessment.

Stacey came back and asked the crowd, "Now ask yourself, how long have you been feeling this way."

My eyes welled up as the lump in my throat struggled to burst; my shallow coughs held the waterworks at bay. I hid my face from the others at the table, pen in hand mimicking a fully engaged note-taker, scribbles pored across the page, attempting to remain invisible. I was supposed to be this powerful, self-assured, successful businesswoman. I knew most of the women in the room; it was only two years before this day when I was one of the presenters on that stage delivering tips on planning and marketing to a crowd just like this one. Did I have it together then, or did I have my true self so buried that my ego tricked my mind possessing my soul and controlling my movements like a puppet? Former and current clients were there; I had to keep it together. What would they think if they saw me run from the room sobbing like a little girl? I wanted to.

I've never felt naked on the outside and raw on the inside, and I was convinced Stacey was talking directly to me. We had never met, but she knew me; every word was exactly what I needed to hear that day. When she finished her presentation, I rushed to the washroom to pack my emotions back in their hiding spot; returning to scout out and find Stacey's table, I had to talk to her. There was a lineup ahead of me, but I knew this was the day my life had to change. What other choice did I have?

A PARADIGM SHIFT

I wanted to know how to leave my husband lovingly and get my business going in the right direction. I wanted to be heard, and I wanted Stacey to lead me down the path to riches. When I first signed up for her program, I felt like mastering my mindset was the back end of the horse, not the front, but I chose to open my mind to what she had to teach us.

This wasn't new territory for me. I had studied mindset, leadership, innovation, quantum physics, and the laws of attraction, and I had read many books on personal and business development for years. My bookshelves overflow with the likes of Napoleon Hill, Brian Tracey, Seth Godin, Eckhart Tolle, and Neile Donald Walsh, to name a few of my favourite thought leaders. I've heard or read many of Stacey's concepts, but working with her as my coach made the information practical and applicable. Rather than intellectualizing everything as before, the teachings moved my head to an experiential feeling in my heart, where real change began. My ego self stepped aside to allow my true self some room to grow and to explore what I would love for my life.

Dad's code took on a new meaning, and I could see the error in "It's God's will." The code, in many situations, was an escape mechanism designed to thwart responsibility for the decisions

I made. I had a new lens into my past, where I learned to dig for the good in everything, and everyone, as a survival tool. Searching for the good became my superpower and my Achilles' heel. It served me and groomed my skills to see beyond the surface with perspectives others couldn't see, and opportunities and insights rose to the surface—a valuable skill when helping clients with their business. The flip side of digging for the good was that it left me wide-open and vulnerable, and God's will turned out to be a handy tool to justify both favourable and unfavourable outcomes.

Working with a life coach, I learned I get to choose what I want, and how life was happening through me and for me, not to me. After a lifetime of programming, I shifted my thinking from trying to figure out the *how* to focusing on the *what*, asking myself, *What will I love?*

Kelly and I were in a dark place, and I saw no way back. I had a realtor scheduled to put a for sale sign on the lawn the week before I met Stacey. We were an inch away from selling the acreage; I wanted out.

Stacey asked me to do one thing. "For thirty days, go ALL in, and each day, make a list of everything you are grateful for, from the small gestures and quirky habits to the bigger things. You love your kitchen with the big windows; Feel your gratitude for all of it."

I cancelled the realtor and did as Stacey suggested, focusing my attention, and expressing gratitude for all the good in our lives. *How ironic,* I thought. *Why is it so difficult for me to dig deep for good in my own life and our marriage when I have spent a lifetime digging deep with others?*

The shift in me had a profound effect on our relationship, and Kelly's behaviour changed. He was relaxed and open to new ideas. We took time to talk and agree on how to communicate with each other, and though we have different values and interests, I learned to accept his.

At dinner one evening, I reached for Kelly's hand, looked into his eyes, and said, "I do love you."

He burst into tears, saying, "That makes me so happy to hear you say those words."

He didn't fuss anymore when I set up my easel in the dining room to take advantage of the natural light pouring in around me. Like my mother pushing her sewing machine to the end of the table to put dinner on for the family, I did the same with my paints, and Kelly took it all in stride.

I was back on stage, delivering insights on marketing and planning, and my talks attracted new, heart-centred clients whose values aligned with my own. Beginning and ending my day with a gratitude practice gave me the foundation and confidence to explore new ideas, and my business and art reaped the benefits. Everything around me took on a deeper and richer meaning, the golden gates opened wide to new possibilities, and "If I can imagine it, I can create it" was my motto.

I concluded that my dad's code was half correct, and like everything in life, there are two sides. Life is a dichotomy, we have a choice, and at the same time, there are no mistakes in life. And my life is a testament, but Dad's code needs to be grounded with intention. Creating a life I love needs a pilot and a co-pilot, and I'm the one flying the plane.

It wasn't only my dad's beliefs I questioned; My spirituality was under a microscope for years. Early in my graphic design career, one of my clients was a Christian newspaper; They paid me $50 for each advertisement I designed, which was considered a reasonable rate in the early '90s. The publisher called and offered to publish a free ad for my company to thank me for all the work I did for them. I felt it appropriate to design an advertisement with a spiritual message; After I submitted it for approval, they called me to come in to discuss my ad.

On the way to their office, I role-played our meeting in my mind, imagining they would commend me for my creative writing skill, and maybe they would ask me to write a column on spirituality. I walked up the stairs to the publisher's office, and five people were sitting on chairs in a semi-circle. They gestured for me to take the empty chair in the middle. They each shared the same stiff, cold expressions; The energy was thick, and I figured out this was not going to be a commendation, more like a condemnation.

The publisher began, "We asked you here to talk about your ad. Can you tell us, please, where you see God?"

To the point—I like that. I replied, "I see God in everything and everyone."

"Do you see God in that tree out there?"

"Yes."

"Do you see God in that rock?"

"Yes, I see God in everything, and I don't just see him; I feel Him. There are so many aspects to God; I am an expression of God as is each one of you."

If they held a buzzer to slap for every wrong answer, each of them would have taken their turn, pouncing with every word that came out of me, and then they'd toss me out the window.

The pastor picked up his Bible, shook it at me and said, "This is the only place you'll find God."

He began to pray for my salvation; The others had their hands in the air, eyes closed, and swaying side to side as the pastor quoted scripture. His words blurred to an unrecognizable drone and trailed off when my attention shifted to the corner, imagining Jesus bursting through the wall in a ray of light. *Is that what's going to happen? Whoa, if it does,* I thought, *maybe he can rescue me from the centre of this circle.* These people were persecuting me.

My design contract ended that day, and we parted ways. I was thankful we weren't living in the 18th century, and I may have told them this. As a left-handed woman who believed God to be life itself, I would indeed have been burned at the stake.

My quest for answers over the years led me to a variety of churches; I was looking for a home, but what I found was a similar problem with each visit. I didn't understand how the minister, priest, or pastor interpreted what they read in scripture. I wondered if they had a book of translations available only to them. In my mind, I'd say to God, "Excuse me, but is this happening?" I was an alien, but I had a relationship with my higher power, so why was this church thing not working? The congregation followed along and appeared to know what the leaders were saying.

It was much like standing at a new exhibit at the art gallery with a group of people staring at a gigantic white canvas with a red dot in the centre. I found the people much more interesting than the art. What was I missing? If I had taken art history, would that painting have revealed a story, or perhaps, like invisible ink, a masterpiece of colour, texture, and expression would burst forth? What did they see that I didn't? Or, did one person stop to wonder, *Why is there a dot on that canvas?* And another person joined to wonder the same, until there were a dozen people too scared to look away for fear that the rest of the crowd might think of them as a peasant?

I took from that painting the word *lonely*. Did the artist intend to send that message? Or, was the intention to capture a group of people who follow the crowd, comfortable in the status quo without any opinion or thought to call their own, feeling very alone as they stare at something they don't understand? How ironic.

My search for spiritual truth came to an end, and I was content with my own belief that life is God and God is life. There wasn't a church that supported my ideas, and half-jokingly, I told friends I'd start my own and call it *The Church of What's Happenin' Now.*

SEGUE

My ego self and my true self had been vying for first place, with my ego doing its best to survive since I was a young girl. We live in a universe of relativity, so we need an opposite perspective to relate the two to understand something. Surviving was my life, and until I could see another way, I couldn't see at all.

I was at a retreat in the mountains with a group of women, laying on the floor and listening to the sounds of Tibetan bowls humming at tones; Some were sweet, and others made my stomach turn. This was my first experience with sound therapy.

When we finished, we gathered around the facilitator who had Gandhi-like serenity beaming from every fibre in her body.

She looked into my eyes, smiled, and softly said, "You don't have to be in control all the time."

I was so taken aback and a little pissed off that she called me out, but that was only because I was embarrassed. I also knew she was right. I had control issues, disguising a self-conscious scaredy-cat trying to present to the world a successful, has-it-all-together woman. The truth was, I didn't have any of my shit together, and the harder I tried, the deeper I dug into the shit hole.

After taking a vacation to Italy with Erika to celebrate our 30/50 birthdays, I turned around and headed back to Italy again, only three weeks later. The tour guide, Giuseppe, who took our group from Rome to Venice, was an entertaining, engaging, and knowledgeable young man with an entrepreneurial spirit. The two of us talked about his passion for starting his own tour business, and I was ripe for a change. He tried a few different start-ups, but he couldn't get the ideas passed by his local officials; He didn't have the affiliates in government he needed to vouch for him. I suggested starting a tour company with the head office in Canada, and we'd run it together, sending Canadians on tours to Italy, and he would be their guide.

I loaded up my new video equipment, and off I went back to Italy to film our upcoming tour, and I'd come home and sell it to Canadians. We started in Rome, and over four days, we made our way to Sienna, Florence, Pisa, Venice, Burano, and Murano, with Naples as an addition to the tour we had taken before. Giuseppe introduced me to Gaeta, a fishing village where he lived with his widowed mother, and I stayed in a villa they owned overlooking the Tyrrhenian Sea. I paused a couple of times to check in with myself. *What the hell are you doing? You don't know this guy, you don't speak the language, and hardly anyone in Italy speaks English; You are an outsider. You could be robbed, killed, and cut up into little pieces and thrown in the sea; No one back home would ever know what happened.*

Giuseppe laughed when I asked if he knew people who made unwanted tourists disappear, and he assured me I was safe travelling with him. I wasn't so sure about this after the train we were on stopped on the track and the conductor told Giuseppe we could be there for hours. Giuseppe told me to grab my stuff and follow him. We hopped onto the train track and ran to the back of the last car.

He said to me, "We are going to cross the track and hop up on the platform on the other side; There is a train scheduled to stop there."

My heart was in my throat as we navigated the four sets of railway tracks; When we got to the platform, I couldn't reach to climb up on my own. Giuseppe grabbed my bags, tossed them behind him, and reached down to hoist me up as a high-speed train flew by within seconds of my rescue. At a maximum speed of 300 km per hour, I didn't hear it coming until the whooshing wind grabbed the tail of my coat and wrapped it around my legs. Fear caught up to me, my heart pounded into my shoulder blades, and my muscles contracted and released with a piercing shot of pain radiating across my lower back.

My mind caught up as the danger passed, and I could take a breath. "Oh my God, we aren't doing that again; I was seconds away from death."

Giuseppe nodded. "Yes, that was a little close." In his broken English. "Many people die every day, and some jump in front of the fast trains on purpose."

Ok, that was not at all reassuring.

He introduced me to his friend who owned a restaurant in Gaeta and only served what he caught the same day. He didn't speak English, and Giuseppe translated. We wanted video shots of the food, wherever we went. In Naples, it was pizza, with Giuseppe narrating the history of pizza. In Gaeta, it was seafood. Giuseppe read and translated each dish at his friend's restaurant and asked me what I would like.

My response was, "All of it, of course." And that is what we got; Everything on the menu was laid out in front of us as I whispered to my new friend, who hadn't quite caught on to my humour yet, "I didn't mean that literally."

We travelled south along the coastline, stopping for short glimpses and video shoots, and Giuseppe was starting to enjoy his time in front of the camera; In true Italian style, his hands were as descriptive as his narration. He took shopkeepers aside in Burano, explaining we were shooting video. Wherever we were, they invited us in to take a video of lace workers in Burano and glass artists in Murano. When we arrived at a grotto, the keeper was at the entrance; He saw the camera and waved for me to leave, no cameras allowed. Again, when Giuseppe told him whatever he said to everyone else, the fellow peered around Giuseppe's shoulder, nodding and smiling at me. He gestured us through with one hand, and he winked at me and covered his eyes with his other hand. He finally confessed and told me he was telling everyone I was a famous filmmaker from Canada, and we were making a movie.

The short time spent in Pompei was burned into me. I held the shaking camera, and I was crying as Giuseppe narrated the story of the catastrophic volcanic eruption of Mount Vesuvius, responsible for the ruins and perfectly preserved remains of mothers swaddling their babies, fathers laying over top of their children as human shields to protect them from the hot ash pouring out of the heavens, men looking to the sky with outstretched arms, and all the horror captured on their faces for two millennia.

We started our company together, sitting at his place, his mother serving cappuccino and pastries. At the same time, I set up our Canadian corporation, settling on the name, *WOW Holidays*, for no other reason than *wow* seemed to be my favourite word on that trip. Once home, I researched the travel industry to discover that this business wasn't going to work. I broke my number one rule by doing the homework after the fun stuff.

We coordinated one trip for a couple, and though they were seasoned travellers, they were mugged at the subway moments after arriving in Rome. He was wearing a money belt, and a group of women and children bumped into them, emptying his belt and zipping it back up in the blink of an eye. Once they replaced their traveller's cheques, they enjoyed their private tour with Giuseppe. However, I decided I didn't want to carry the liability or responsibility of people travelling from Canada, and Giuseppe bought me out of the company.

This was a great adventure, but from the moment I entered the subway on my own in Rome, my soul had called in every guardian to watch over me at every step. Once the adventure ended, I knew the business wasn't for me, but I was deeply grateful for the experience.

Starting businesses was a distraction, and it was an exercise that kept my ego self fed, while my true self was buried deep, nudging me to slow down and listen, and urging me to stop living in the future.

OUT OF MY MIND

The fog lifted as I continued my journey with Stacey's guidance and coaching. I was learning to master my mindset, building a bridge between my mind and my spirit, and affirming there are no mistakes in this life. I was co-creating, with God as my co-pilot. I knew it. I felt it.

This internal work prepared me for the life-altering event that welcomed me at the start of 2019. I expected to launch the new program we'd worked at for months. Erika put her Master's in Communications to good use as my writer and editor. Rheagan helped build the digital platform for an online training program to teach small business owners to create a value-centred business plan. Everything was on track until the train came. Oh, the trains in my life just keep on rolling.

I had a biopsy the first week of January, and it took until March for the results. I knew something wasn't right with my body, and I'd waited for months just to get in to see the oncologist for a biopsy. Putting my mindset lessons into practice, I focused on the present and whether I was playing with my grandchildren, attending a network meeting, facilitating a workshop, or standing in a grocery line talking with the clerk, my mission was to give something of value. I became acutely aware of time, and aware how, with each passing moment gone the minute I experienced them, every moment after became an opportunity to do with it what *I wanted.*

I thought about how fortunate I was to have been doing what I love for a living because so many people exchange time for a paycheque, and they don't like their job. Here I am creating, developing, teaching, painting, writing, and helping other people follow their passion. I felt like the wealthiest woman in the world.

Kelly and I booked a trip to Cabo for the week of my birthday, and we were flying out four days after Dr. Wells called with the biopsy results; I had cancer.

I thought I was ready to hear it, but the word cancer seemed surreal when spoken in a sentence with my name attached to it. Instantly, I became aware of my mortality; Knowing it and realizing it are not the same, and now I realized, I wouldn't be here forever. *OMG, I have an expiry date.*

"My husband and I are booked to fly out to Mexico next week."

"Go on your holiday. We will send you a letter with the appointment details, and we can discuss your options then. Enjoy your time in Mexico." Dr. Wells sounded confident.

Does she always say that with such confidence, or does she reserve that tone for patients who have minor cancer? Is there such a thing as minor cancer? I wondered.

Ok, I said to myself, *I KNOW nothing happens by accident, and I have choices. Up to this moment, as far back as I can remember, every event, circumstance, person I've met, married, dated, friended, or un-friended all happened because of the choices I've made. What are my options at this moment? What reality do I want to create?*

My logical brain took the lead, taking inventory of the tools I had to work with. I went to my bookshelf, closed my eyes, and reached for a book, trusting my choice would guide me. The perfect answer revealed itself when I opened my eyes to see I had pulled out the timeless classic, *The Power of Now* by Eckhart Tolle. Living in the moment. Of course. I didn't have to do or plan anything except live in each moment. I instantly knew the lesson I was meant to learn, instead of it slapping me in hindsight with an "aha" moment after the fact. Hindsight was no longer my teacher; I was the creator of each moment and vowed to live in each moment with love and gratitude.

Kelly and I boarded the plane, and as my foot hit the tarmac in Mexico, I paused. The air was warm and sweet, just like before when I was there with my siblings, and the moment belonged to me.

We traded our timeshare week in Arizona for the week in Cabo San Lucas, unaware that the prices on pretty much everything was more like being in Hawaii. *Oh well, this may be my last trip anywhere, so worth every cent*, I decided.

We checked in; Our resort was a combination between an all-inclusive and a dig-deep-in-your-wallet resort. It was beautiful; Our villa was adobe-style and familiar. My sister and I had watched an adobe home builder in Honduras making stone blocks by hand, in a wheelbarrow, on a 40-degree afternoon. This type of house was built by hand, one handmade block at a time.

Kelly and I dropped our bags and went for a walk through the resort and down to the beach, where we discovered the waves along that side were too strong for swimming. We looked at each other and smiled. On the water or by the water suited us just fine, but something we do have in common is neither of us like swimming.

Reviewing the menu outside the first restaurant, I commented how I should have done some homework. The menu they emailed us before leaving home gave us an option for all-inclusive for $200 US per day, per person. It seemed outrageous pricing for

Mexico. We opted out, but the menu staring back at us gave us a new budget for our trip; The all-inclusive menu would have been a much better deal.

We booked a sunset dinner cruise and hang gliding, and my favourite by far was the dune buggies. The waiver was extensive, and an ambulance was outside the front door. There were three other couples in the group, and our tour guide enthusiastically introduced himself. We were each given a side-by-side dune buggy; Our guide told us that the trails were through the bush, over steep hills, and on the beach, and that we'd take a break halfway through for refreshments.

He asked each couple, "Which one is driving?"

He came to us, and Kelly pointed to me.

The guide shook his head, "No, no, this is too dangerous. You have to drive."

Kelly insisted I was driving, and the guide shrugged his shoulders and commented about one person being taken out by ambulance earlier in the day.

Behind the wheel, I was free, full-throttle through the bush, taking flight at the top of hills, and spinning donuts in the sand. The guide looked back at his group to watch us launching from the hilltop in flight, laughing until my stomach muscles were sore; I was having the time of my life. Poor Kelly suffers from motion sickness, but he held out to the halfway point when we stopped for a bottle of water.

The guide came over when we pulled up. "I am so sorry I underestimated you're driving skill, my apologies. You are one crazy señora."

He walked back to the group.

Kelly put his arm around me and squeezed me, saying, "Good job, honey."

He slid into the driver's seat for the final leg of the tour.

Kelly was having a nap the afternoon of my birthday, and I put a dress on and went down to the martini bar overlooking the beach. I sat at a high-top table, scanning my surroundings, taking in every colour and smell. When I closed my eyes and listened, I could feel the power of the waves crashing into rocks below. Live jazz music was playing in the restaurant next door. I was at peace, *even though this may be my last birthday*, I thought as the bartender greeted me and passed me a menu.

I glanced at it. "Oh yes, of course, this is a martini bar, and this is a martini menu," I quipped. "I've never had one, so let's start at the top and work our way down."

I went back in my mind to my thought when I first sat down. *This may be my last birthday.* How is this different than any other birthday? We don't know from moment to moment whether an aneurism will take us out or a meteorite will push us off our axis and obliterate the entire planet. We just don't know, so why does it take a diagnosis like cancer to realize all we have is this moment?

I thought about my time, as a young girl, looking up at the sky, contemplating layer after layer of stars to what end? There is no end; How can there be? If there was, what is on the other side? Nothing is something.

My second martini was chocolate. Well, that's like having dessert first. What was my soul calling me to do? Never mind, order number three on the menu, a French Martini, and by my fourth, it was time to text Kelly to save me from the fifth so we could walk next door for dinner.

Earlier in the day, we were at the beach with an opportunity to buy a plethora of things I didn't need. I stopped the man selling Cuban cigars.

"How much for one?" I asked.

He wanted me to buy the entire box, and I said, "Listen, I don't smoke; I just want one cigar. It's my birthday, and I've never smoked a stogey before."

I hadn't smoked cigarettes since October 20th, 2007 when I gave up my pack-and-a-half a day habit. He conceded, and I paid him $20 for one cigar; Kelly and I went back to the martini bar for a lighter and instructions on how to light the thing.

The beach had a wooden walkway with lanterns strung overhead, stretching across the sand from the restaurant to the end of the resort. We held hands and walked, and I smoked my cigar.

THE GOLDEN GATES

When we returned from Cabo, I assessed my business, asking what I would love to do next. I didn't have a clear answer, and my appointment at the Cross Cancer Institute defined the next few months for me; I just had to go with the flow.

Dr. Wells was the cardiologist who did the biopsy, and we were joined by Dr. Ceterra, the radiologist on her team. I had two choices: surgery or radiation. Dr. Wells would perform the surgery, and she explained what that would entail. Dr. Ceterra was a little more enthusiastic than I was comfortable with as she described the process and the potential side effects from thirty rounds of radiation.

I put my hand up and announced, "Door number one, please."

I was booked and prepped, and, in the meantime, I would keep busy with the projects I'd committed to before my diagnosis. I was designing two magazines, due in August, and I was grateful to have something creative to put my energy into.

Since my surgery was on a warm Friday in May and golf season was in full swing, it crossed my mind that Dr. Wells may be a golfer; I know, I was quick to stereotype. Well, avid golfers in our area ring out every drop of sunlight and tee time our short season has to offer. I didn't want to be rushed through as the final patient of the week taking up her valuable time on the greens. When she came into the operating room, she put her hand on my shoulder and asked how I was doing.

I said, "You know what? I'm great because you are a master at what you do, and this surgery is going to be your best work ever." I was projecting my subliminal message to Dr. Wells to take her time. I thought maybe planting the seed would pre-pave a perfect outcome.

She replied, "Hmmm, ok. Let's do this."

I woke to Kelly sitting in a chair, reading a magazine at the end of the bed. My legs were wrapped in inflatable bags attached to a compressor. My thighs felt the firm hug every thirty seconds as the bags expanded and contracted.

"Hi, honey."

"You're awake!" Kelly put his magazine on the chair and tip-toed over to kiss me. "How are you doing?"

"I'm good. Why are you whispering? Is that like turning the radio down to find an address? What are these bags for? Have you talked to the doctor to see how everything went? When can I go home?"

He smiled. "I don't know. The doctor hasn't been in . . ." he said, halting our talk when the nurse came in.

"Well, hello, it's great to see you're awake." She checked the spacesuit I was wearing and my vitals. "How are you feeling?"

"Good, thank you. What are these bags for? Have you talked to the doctor to see how everything went? When can I go home?"

"Everything went well according to your chart. The bags are to give your lymphatic system a little help after surgery."

"How long do I have to wear them?"

"Only until you are up and walking around. You will be here for a few days, and a doctor will be by to check on you later today or tomorrow."

"I have to pee," I said, gesturing to Kelly for help.

I decided I would wait for the effects from the anesthetic to wear off before sprinting down the hall, but that evening, Kelly and I took a stroll. The nurse was shocked to see me up so soon; She said most of her patients would stay in bed for three days before trying.

"I don't want to wear Michelin Man pants any longer than I have to, and I want to go home as soon as I can."

Every moment after surgery, I took a concerted effort, looking after my incisions where they extracted one lymph node on the top of my thigh on both sides. I was happy to learn there was only one incision; That meant the cancer was contained and hadn't travelled.

Amy was an incredible help, taking time off work to stay with me. Kelly was out of town three days a week, and when he was home, he shied away from the caregiving role. Not because he didn't want to; He just didn't know what to do.

As I healed, I ordered a stand-up desk to get back to the computer to work on the magazines. I was not one to sit idle; Besides, I had deadlines, and deadlines have a great way of focusing the mind. I maintained my pre-surgery commitment to live in the moment and focus on the now. When I was in pain and couldn't sit, I would pause to acknowledge my gratitude for everything in my life. When my mind drifted to future events or concocted negative dialogue, something most of us do throughout our day, I noticed my thoughts, redirecting them back to the moment. My morning ritual helped with the post-surgery recovery, but most of all it fueled my creativity, which I poured into my projects.

I was eager to meet with Dr. Wells for my follow-up, and when I walked into the examination room to see both Dr. Wells and Dr. Ceterra come in, I braced myself for the news.

"Surgery went well, but we couldn't get it all without causing permanent damage, and you would likely need a colostomy bag if I went any further. I consulted with Dr. Ceterra . . ."

The two nodded to each other.

"You will need to have radiation after all."

Dr. Ceterra explained that her team works together to create a radiation plan; I would need to come in every day for treatments once they were scheduled.

"How many treatments?" I asked through my tears, the first I had shed since my surgery.

"Once we have the plan, we will know for sure, but I can confidently say between twenty-five and thirty-two."

She went on to talk about the side effects to expect; The external burns would begin after two weeks of treatment and spike two weeks after the final radiation treatment.

"Oh, joy," I replied. "I was hoping I wouldn't have to go this route, but here we are. When do we begin?"

I received my very first tattoos on my radiation plan day when Dr. Ceterra gave me my schedule and marked six dots on my torso; These were to provide the setpoints for the technicians to line me up under the radiation machine that spun around my body, under the metal table for five minutes, each day for twenty-eight days.

The Cross Cancer Institute became my second home. Starting the second week of August, every weekday at 4:00 p.m., I went to the locker, put on the blue gown that I finally figured out how to tie, and sat in the waiting room. Each day, a gentleman resembling my former husband Nick sat across from me. I must talk to people; I can't not talk, which is likely why total strangers overshare personal details with me, no matter where I am. Grocery clerks enjoy filling me in on problems with their kids or husbands. I've put my poser therapist hat on several times while my peppers and tomatoes made their way across the scanner. My mom told me I have an invisible sign on my forehead that reads, "YOU CAN TELL ME ANYTHING."

The gentleman's name was Frank, a millwright/pipefitter. *My God,* I thought. *He is Nick's double.* He looked like him, talked like him, and had the same job as him. Frank's kids took his dog, his wife left him, and he worked with a bunch of assholes that didn't care if he lived or died.

Well, we started on a positive note. That was my inside sarcastic voice.

I looked at him empathetically and asked, "Do you want to live or die? That's all that matters here."

He looked at me for a moment and slowly shook his head. "I don't even know anymore. I have to do thirty-five rounds of this radiation, and then internal radiation, where they put radioactive beads inside of me. I can't have anyone around me while this is going on, so it doesn't matter that my dog is gone since he can't be with me anyway."

As the fixer that I am, I told him about a couple of books that I was happy to share. "They will give you another perspective to focus on."

He interrupted me. "No, I don't read any of THAT stuff."

I was called in for my treatment, and from then on, Frank purposely sat in a chair at the other end of the room, avoiding any chance I might have something positive to say to him.

I walked in for my last treatment on September 18th with boxes of homemade Italian sweets from my catering friend and put them on the counter for the technicians.

"Thank you for all you've done for me."

I had my treatment and walked over to the wall where I had watched dozens of patients triumphantly ring the bell, signalling their last treatment—a profoundly emotional moment for most, and mine was no exception. I picked a handbell off the table in one hand and, with the other, reached for the leather tassel hanging from the wall bell. As hard I could, I swung them both as everyone in the waiting room clapped and cheered.

Just as the doctor had said, the burns began to peak two weeks following my final treatment. My legs were raw, and every morning was an excruciating exercise to move from my bed to the coffee maker and then outside to the verandah. I preferred my solitude when recovering from surgery and radiation, primarily to maintain my positive focus.

My mom knew this and never used the sympathetic tone when we talked or when she came for a visit to deliver her regular care package of homemade bread, relishes, and groceries she offered to pick up. She always had a pie or something sweet for Kelly.

Every day, he'd ask how I was doing, and I would respond with "Every day is a new day, and I'm getting better."

He was never one to talk about his feelings, and I didn't know anything was ever bothering him until he'd blow up at something petty and utterly unrelated to what was going on at the time.

One day, he watched as I shuffled from my recovery bed to the kitchen and poured a coffee. He walked over and gave me a long, firm hug. He began to cry, brushing away tears beneath his glasses.

"I am so scared," he finally blurted out. "You have been through so much, and I'm scared to lose you. You never complain about what you're going through. I have never met a stronger person."

I wouldn't allow Kelly to see the results of my treatments. The sight of blood made him woozy, and if he saw what was happening to my skin, he wouldn't have handled it well. Every morning revealed new radiation burns, red and raw, seeping to the surface from inside my body. I knew it was coming, and I had the creams, ointments, pain medication, and selective cotton garments to allow my delicate skin exposure to air so it could breathe back to health. But it took time. Weeks went by before I could walk without straddling the invisible saddle or sit on a chair without the aid of a foam donut.

It was the morning of Halloween, and I was looking forward to dinner at Erika's and trick-or-treating with the kids in the evening. From my office, I heard the shower running. Kelly was getting ready for work when I was on my 9:00 a.m. call with a client. A half-hour into our conversation, Kelly came into my office holding his chest.

"Sorry to interrupt. I'm in a lot of pain."

"OMG, I have to go. My husband is having a heart attack."

I followed him to the front door, firing questions and suggesting we call an ambulance.

"Just take me to the hospital. The way you drive, that will be quicker."

We could have gone to the large hospital in south Edmonton, a huge facility with a waiting room that never seems to empty. We chose the community hospital in Sherwood Park where we knew he would get immediate care. We were greeted by the emergency staff, who took him straight into the back, laid him on a stretcher, and had me sit at admitting to give the admitting clerk Kelly's details.

"You drove him?"

"Yes."

"Has he ever had a heart attack?"

"No, but his dad died from a heart attack, but he was a smoker and a drinker, and Kelly doesn't do any of that. He is healthy."

While the admitting clerk questioned and typed, I watched over her shoulder as they hooked him up to an ECG machine and scurried him into another room. She told me I could join him, and I stood out of the way of the hurried staff whose calm conversation with Kelly contrasted with their swift hands tearing packaging from syringes and plugging cords into machines attached to the rounds taped to Kelly's chest.

One intern was reading the operating manual for one of the machines to confirm the procedures and explained Kelly would be transported to the city where they have cardiac specialists. They gave him a shot of nitroglycerin and prepped him for the ambulance ride to the University Hospital in Edmonton.

He was awake and alert when I asked him how he was feeling.

"Since they gave me that shot, I feel great. I could go to work right now."

"Ya, no, that's not happening," I responded in my scary, motherly tone.

He asked that I call his boss, who was shocked to hear this was Kelly and not one of his other drivers having a heart attack. Kelly was in good physical shape, a non-smoker, and had only the occasional rum and coke—and I mean occasional. He always said I made up for it.

He had already been moved into his semi-private room at the hospital by the time I arrived with his bag of toiletries I liked to call his makeup bag. He was now in the care of the top heart surgeons in the country. I waited with him until he was taken for an MRI to determine the extent of damage to his heart. The cardiologist inserted stents in two blocked arteries through a tube in his arm.

I found it remarkable how fast the procedure was; He was back in his room within an hour. I sat in the only guest chair, made of wooden arms and legs and with a red leather-covered rock posing as a cushion. It was bad enough that I was still struggling to sit with remnants of my burns, but this chair was designed for people to leave long before visiting hours were over.

On his last night in the hospital, I brought my dinner to join him while he insisted on eating the food he chose off the menu that morning. We talked about the challenging year we'd been through and how incredible 2020 was going to be.

THE PEASANT

How we see ourselves is often a refection from the outside, influenced by other people's opinions, remarks, and sometimes, one simple comment will wedge itself in the recesses of our minds and hang out for years. In my experience, corporations attract ego-driven executives whose leadership skills haven't grown much beyond the sandbox. I know this isn't the case in all corporate environments, but when I look back at my time working for a particular company, it's clear where my confidence was shaken.

The human resources department was quiet and unwelcoming. I never understood why I reported to them when I was managing the graphics department; It seemed fitting to be working under the marketing team. I didn't know anyone on the marketing team or if there was an actual marketing department. I was told there was. It was odd that I worked directly with the presidents of each division, and they didn't seem to have much of a plan to share, only off-the-cuff ideas. Perhaps, it was like Harriet, the fictional assistant my mom and I created so we could jokingly blame her, saying to each other when something went south, "It *must* have been Harriet."

Four women were working in the HR department: Carol, the manager, and her assistant, Donna; Kathy, who we called the Grim Reaper since she was responsible for firing people; and Susan, the receptionist. Susan was friendlier than the bunch, except when the other women were present; Her demeanour shifted in sync to match theirs—cold and unapproachable. I reported directly to Carol, constantly feeling like I was under a microscope in her presence. Her off-handed comments were berating.

"Is that your nightgown?" she asked one morning.

I returned the compliment the following day when she came to work wearing a blue knit top with a raised white poodle design on the shoulder. "Are those your pyjamas?"

She and I had a strange relationship, hot and cold, and I was never too sure whether she liked me. For instance, after a stern talk about the people I befriended at work and how it could negatively impact my career, I found a small treasure chest ornament on my desk, with a card attached that read: *From your friend, Carol.* I never knew how to take her and did my best to respond to her with humour. When she announced that she was going on a holiday, she asked if I would take care of her plant, her unhealthy azalea. Before she returned, I replaced the original with a fresh, lush azalea, twice the size of the sickly one. She seemed to appreciate it, but I couldn't read her.

Her assistant, Donna, commissioned me to paint a mural in the wine room they added during their home renovation. When Carol heard this, she asked if I would paint a large floral in watercolour, but it had to be large; Her outstretched arms suggested thirty-six inches wide. We booked a time for her to come by my place to look at some of my work, including the watercolour I had started for her.

I set up paintings on easels, side by side in the living room, showcasing acrylics on canvas and a few small watercolours I was particularly fond of. One of the watercolours earned me a spot in a juried gift show the month before. A man had walked up to one of my bright acrylic paintings of a friendly frog I brought to draw people into my booth at the show.

He studied it for a minute or two and said, "Interesting, you have two very different styles going on in here." And then he abruptly walked away.

What does that mean? Is that a good thing? I didn't know and figured it wasn't relevant since I hadn't sold anything while sitting at the show for three days. Like several non-juried shows before, not one sale to speak of, so I was a wounded bird by the time my boss stepped into my living room to examine my work.

She walked from one painting to the next, without a word, and moved to the in-progress watercolour I was working on for her.

She quipped, "Your work is certainly dark, isn't it?"

"What do you mean?"

"Oh, the subjects aren't dark." She twirled her index finger in front of my chest. "You must have something dark going on in there."

She thanked me and left. It all happened so fast. I cleaned my house for her, borrowed easels to present my work professionally, and created small tags with made-up, exciting names for each piece, and made-up prices I plucked from the sky, since I didn't know how to price my art. I sat in the middle of my living room floor, cross-legged, resting my chin in my hands, looking at each of my creations, and I cried. I shifted from confusion to anger. *What did that comment even mean? What is dark about these paintings? They're bright, but not dark. What was it the guy meant by two styles he saw in my frog painting?* I was confused. Carol threw another emotional curveball at me, no doubt to keep me in my place, and I was angry with myself for rushing out to buy a $300 roll of watercolour paper I couldn't afford.

I had already started the mural in Donna's basement, working on it over two weekends. It took everything in me to brush off my recent failures, and my fear that my "internal darkness" might reflect my feelings in Donna's mural, giving Carol more to criticize. *Zen, Shauna. Zen!*

While I was painting, I saw Donna so seldom that I often wondered whether I was alone in the house, until the day I was finishing up. She came down to talk to the electrician across the hallway who was unpacking his tools to begin wiring the pot lights. They were leaving the room together when I greeted the two, catching Donna off guard—an awkward moment when she had to make introductions.

She introduced him to me, saying, "This is my, um . . . friend, Shauna," almost swallowing her words.

I wasn't her friend; There was no way either she or Carol would consider me anywhere near their class of people, whatever they thought their class level to be. I was beneath them. I didn't measure up to be called anything but an employee who happened to paint on the side. I was a peasant by their standards. I was initially hired in a temporary position to help with the overflow of work, so my resume wasn't necessary. If they knew my level of education amounted to a spattering of classes past Grade 9 and I was self-taught from there on, I wouldn't have made it through the front door. It was my people skills and the fact that I was a competent designer that earned me the full-time position. I won numerous "above and beyond" awards with the company and earned the respect from our internal clients, but I never felt like one of them, nor did I want to.

My art career froze solid in that wine room, and my confidence remained cross-legged on the floor of my living room, long after I sold the house. I gave every painting away, except for the watercolour that earned me a spot in the gift show. I followed the path that continued to present itself, the business route; It felt familiar and safe, and it was lucrative. Companies always needed graphic design, and as I expanded my services into marketing and business planning, clients needed those services too—but my soul craved more. Our gallery was the closest I came to living my passion, but that nagging whisper of "You're not good enough" kept me on the other side of the counter, focused on the other artist's work. Another twelve years would pass before I learned the secret to living a life I love.

THE MOTHER
OF ALL CAREERS

"You work too much."

"Says who?"

"Says other people and me. You do. You work every day, including weekends."

"But I don't consider it work, so really, I'm a lazy bum," I responded to Kelly's out-of-the-blue critique.

"You are your boss. Do what you want."

"I am doing what I want, but to be honest, my clients are the boss, and when they need something, I have to give it to them. Making hay while the sun shine's, baby. I'll bring it up at the next staff meeting."

"You don't have any staff."

"I don't need other people to have a staff meeting, and I'll take your suggestions under advisement."

What I've done for a living and why has evolved. I am in awe of lifers, spending entire working years with one company or even the same career. Kelly is a lifer; He hopped in one of his father's semi-trucks directly out of high school. He's worked for different companies, but he's always driven trucks. If I ask him if he loves his job, he looks puzzled that I would ask such a question.

I've changed jobs more times than I can count, and considering I've been self-employed since 1988, that's quite a few jobs before and between my ventures. My business evolved out of necessity, and the ideas that failed weren't actual failures in my mind. I had an idea and saw it through to discover it wasn't for me, so I don't consider it a failure. I fear regret far more than I fear failure.

The decision to be a mother trumps any other decision I've made in business or life. I consider motherhood a career fit for warrior queens; We learn to navigate and triumph on the battleground of life, to protect and train our successors. I grew up with my children, I was twenty when Erika was born, and I knew little about anything. I believe she had at least one angel follow her through her formative years, and I had two.

Erika was the catalyst for change; My party years were over and would likely have killed me if I hadn't met Kelly and gotten pregnant. Having the responsibility for someone else seemed easier than looking after myself. By the time Amy arrived, Erika was running circles around me, and together they defined my job as a mom. I was determined to give them the tools I developed in life, not those I learned growing up when kids were meant to be seen and not heard.

There weren't aisles filled with books on parenting in bookstores like today. Parenting was an exercise in trial and error, and I thought the first child prepared me for the second; I was wrong. Erika and Amy may have been raised in the same home, but the only thing they've ever had in common is their mother.

Since I volunteered at the school in both Erika's and Amy's classes, their teachers and I became friends, and they supported me with advice and insights on what to do and what not to do. Without sharing names, they weren't shy about telling me horror stories students shared with them or about the overbearing parents who wouldn't stay home, forever underfoot and telling the teachers how to do their jobs.

I was aghast to hear Erika was the first to step up in class and help the teacher or tutor another student; I had to plead with both girls to do anything at home. Children are different people in the company of their parents; Their true selves are revealed once they walk out the front door.

The teachers commended me as being a good role model for the girls, teaching them how to treat others and respect adults. Both girls were independent and loving by nature. They stood up for themselves and others.

I struggled to balance work and time with them, but I loved them, and they knew it. I wrote inspiration notes tucked in their lunch bags. Sometimes, I'd pile on the lipstick and seal the letter with a kiss. I was more concerned that they felt loved than whether they could cook or do laundry. Expressing love and compassion was paramount, something I craved as a child; My mother loved us, but she struggled to express affection, something she adopted from her mother.

The girls never knew how little money we had, and I wanted to keep it that way, out of fear they would develop a poverty mentality. Digging through the couch cushions for change to buy milk wasn't something I wanted them to see.

I learned to budget, but there were times when we needed groceries, and the bank account was empty. I relied on government assistance for a few months, receiving $700 for the month. Our rent was $375, leaving little else to cover utilities and food, much less extracurricular activities for the girls. The community had a volunteer program for parents to earn credits toward city programs. I took full advantage, volunteering for everything I could so the girls could take lessons and attend camps.

"We'll make one" was the mantra in our house. The girls wanted a fireplace at Christmas to hang their stockings on, so we painted a fireplace on rolls of paper leftover from the backdrop I did each year for the school. The girls rolled brown paper, tied at each end, brushed brown paint along the folds to represent bark, and we glued the logs to the fireplace on the wall.

Project management needed polishing, especially when it came to school projects.

"Mom, I have to build a solar system for science."

"When is it due?"

"Tomorrow."

Erika would fall asleep on the couch while I stayed up until 3:00 a.m. to finish her solar system.

And I always had surprise baking projects to complete before I went to bed: "Mom, I need cupcakes for the class tomorrow."

My own projects filled the house, the drafting table took up the dining room, and illustrations were taped across the walls for the Bird Book; I partnered with a bird enthusiast to create a workbook for Grades 4 to 6. We sold it to the school system as a concept, and I designed the book and drew the birds from photos I found in library books. The girls worked around boxes of paper and signage that stretched from the dining room to the patio doors. They adjusted to my chaos and took most of it in stride.

Erika started her first job as a bus girl at a local Denny's when she was fifteen. Her taste in clothing far exceeded my budget, so we had a deal. I put in what I would pay for jeans, and if she wanted the designer jeans, she had to foot the bill for the rest. She and Amy developed an excellent money sense and paid their way through post-secondary school and car purchases, and Erika bought her first house while in university and working as a server at a restaurant.

There was collateral damage whenever I remarried. Orville was mean to Erika, and Nick was mean to Amy. I harboured the guilt for years, and there's still a sting that accompanies some memories. Communication and trust were cornerstones with the girls. Therefore, I felt it was important to tell them the story about putting little Rosemary up for adoption and why. Waiting until I thought they were old enough for the news, I took them to lunch once each reached the age of sixteen to share my story.

Ironically, on Mother's Day in 2015, the girls took me for lunch, and I told them, "I have something to tell you two."

Simultaneously, they blurted, "You're pregnant!" teasing and laughing at their knack for catching me off guard.

"No, I'm not pregnant, brats. Remember I told you about little Rosemary? Well, she contacted me."

By their expressions, I was relieved I had told them years before.

Their reactions were worlds apart.

Amy was mortified and angry. "No, no, you're MY mom, no."

And Erika was quiet. I could see the wheels turning as her sister continued her hissy fit, and she said little more than "Wow, that's something."

Reminding Amy several times in the conversation that this wasn't about her, I told them her name was now Sylvia. She was married to a man named Nathan, and they lived in Ontario. That was all I volunteered for information, leaving it with them to process.

Sylvia and I talked a few times by phone, acquainting each other with snippets from thirty years as strangers, and it helped to settle my emotions. I wasn't clear on how to approach this new relationship. From the time I read Nathan's email, a range of emotions clouded my ability to figure out what the next steps should be. Nathan wanted to do an extensive public reveal with

Sylvia's and my meeting. I disagreed and told him I didn't like those public displays on TV. Besides, what if we don't like each other—a real possibility. She may be my biological child, but we've lived separate lives.

She and Nathan were planning a trip to Calgary for a wedding, and I set up an evening to drive down with my mom and meet them for dinner. As we approached the restaurant, she was unmistakably my daughter. We faced each other, staring for a moment or two, and embraced, laughing, and commenting on the uncanny resemblance between us. She looked like a younger version of me.

We met Nathan and their three-year-old son, Seth. Nathan was a nurse in the military, and Sylvia was a chef for the top brass in Ottawa. She loved to paint, left-handed like me, and I told her of the incredible cooks in our family—a passion we all shared thanks to my grandma. Sylvia said she had the picture I drew and the poem I wrote for her when she was born, and they've hung on her wall ever since.

I felt I needed to explain why I put her up for adoption when I raised two girls, and she hadn't been included; This was a pain point for me. She assured me that she never felt abandoned, and her mom told her all about me when she was young. She and Nathan expressed admiration and gratitude for my choice, agreeing there was divinity at play that brought her mom and me together. Knowing Sylvia was doing so well filled a void I didn't think I had until I met her.

Like bumpers in a bowling alley, being a mother to Erika and Amy kept me pointed in the right direction as they grew up; They were the wind beneath my sails. There is a stigma around being a single parent, seen as a second-class citizen, dependent on the system, with little hope of making it out of the trenches. That's how I felt people looked upon me, fueling me to work harder.

My passion to be an artist never waned, even when the opinions of others shook my confidence and put my art career on hold.

Regardless of where we are, our past does not dictate our future. What we do today paves the future according to our thoughts, feelings, and actions. Letting go of the past and reprogramming my beliefs from "I don't know if I can" to "I know I can" has been the most challenging and rewarding shift and daily practice. We can't take a lifetime of mental habits and expect them to change without putting in the work to create new patterns. It's simple, but it isn't easy.

My intention and motivation set me apart from the single mothers who sat in my class to learn how to start a business when it was the government benefits that lured them, not their business idea. The intention to be the best person I can be and the motivation to give my girls a head start in life was my job and the best one I've had so far, but it may be trumped by being a grandma. The jury is out on that.

THREE SECRETS

It's not rocket science, but it's taken more than fifty years to learn what should be at the core of our education system from the first day a child enters the front door.

Secret number one:
The answer isn't out there.

Seeking approval from my parents, my teachers, and my bosses only served to reinforce my inadequacies. Our system is upside-down. I was given a gift from a student in one of my workshops that changed my perspective on life and business.

I was contracted to deliver a marketing workshop to an Indigenous group of business owners. When I arrived at the slide with a graphic of Maslow's hierarchy of needs, the energy shifted in the room. The participants were exchanging glances with each other.

Maslow's theory is based on five categories of human needs:

- First is **physiological needs**—food, clothing, shelter.
- Second is **safety needs**—personal security, employment health.

- Third is **love and belonging**—emotional connection, relationships.
- Fourth is **esteem needs**—self-esteem, achievement.
- And finally, fifth is **self-actualization needs**—personal growth, potential.

After I finished explaining the hierarchy, I asked the room what they thought about this because a few were whispering and nodding with each, and I mentioned the energy shift in the room. They explained that in their culture, the pyramid in my example is upside-down, where self-actualization is their first basic need. I sat down and listened as my workshop evolved into a group conversation. This paradigm shift took me off my feet and forced me to review what I've been taught in business, and I changed the business planning program I developed to align with this new paradigm. This secret was hiding in plain view, and I came to understand a greater truth. The only way we will survive as a race is if we stop looking outside of ourselves for answers, as the internal work precedes everything.

There is a natural flow of energy and growth when our priority is **self-actualization**: personal and creative growth, which leads to the next level of **esteem needs**, where self-confidence and self-respect give us a lens into other people's perspectives, triggering the next level of **love and belonging needs**, where friendship, intimacy, and trust naturally leads to **safety needs**, where our sense of personal and financial security naturally takes care of our last level of needs, **physiological needs** which is food, shelter, and clothing.

When we begin with ourselves, we right our world from the inside, out.

Secret number two:
Imposter Syndrome is a good thing.

There sure are a lot of syndromes these days, and for every symptom, there is a label. ADHD wasn't a thing when I was young, and now, so many around me talk about it, are medicated for it, and I have it too. I've always known about my lack of attention, and I'm accustomed to Surel the squirrel who has taken up residence in my office and scoots across my desk. ADHD is not a bad thing. They call it Attention-Deficit Hyperactivity Disorder; I call it creativity. Why does everything have to have a negative connotation to it? This is my perspective: I think acceptance goes a long way to fixing what isn't necessarily broken. Imposter Syndrome has been tossed around as though it's another disorder that needs to be fixed. We are so accustomed to labels, we don't look below the surface to consider another viewpoint. I am the queen of Imposter Syndrome. What is it? I laughed when I googled the term and found questions, such as:

- Is Imposter Syndrome a mental illness?
- What triggers Imposter Syndrome?
- How do you fix Imposter Syndrome?
- What are the five types of Imposter Syndrome?

I laughed because it's been my partner my entire adult life, and it's taken me up until now to understand the simplicity of it.

It is defined as "a phenomenon . . . experienced equally by men and women and frequently coexists with depression and anxiety."[1]

---

1   Crystal Raypole, "You're Not a Fraud. Here's How to Recognize and Overcome Imposter Syndrome," Online article, Healthline, April 16, 2021, https://www.healthline.com/health/mental-health/imposter-syndrome.

Someone even attached five subcategories to the syndrome: the Perfectionist, the Superwoman/man, the Natural Genius, the Soloist, and the Expert.[2]

My non-clinical observation is this: It feels much better to be good at what we do, but as we grow, we step into new, unfamiliar territory, and the uncertainty we feel is magnified when we don't understand—this feeling is natural. Our first reaction is to label our feelings, and when we place a label like Imposter Syndrome on them, fear overrides the benefits of uncertainty. Imposter Syndrome lives on the edge of growth, and rather than viewing it as a negative quality we think we have, we can embrace it and acknowledge the fact that we are growing. I don't think true imposters have a problem with their identity—they know who they are.

Secret number three:
Our past is not who we are.

My fears of what people might think of me being married four times, or what family would say about me sharing my story, or how people would judge me when they learned I was a high school dropout, are the ghosts from my past that held tightly onto my ankles, refusing to let me move forward. But when I finally put it all on paper, I could see the bigger picture, affirming to me it has all been purposeful and deliberate. And though I wasn't always successful at it, my intention has been to live and contribute in my own way, harmoniously. If I am doing the best with what I have, there is no need to look outside of myself, hold onto the past, or worry that I am not whom people think I am. At some point, we will all get to where we don't give a shit, and hopefully, it happens while we are vertical.

---

2   Ibid.

I believe no matter what others do to us, we can move past it. What's the alternative? We must let go in order to live a life we love. I've learned the best way to let go is to decide for myself: Who is the greatest version of me? What am I doing as that person? And who is coming along for the ride? When that became clear, the fear evaporated, and I picked up my paintbrush and said goodbye with gratitude to the comfort zone that protected me, fed me, and groomed me. I am now grateful to be back in my studio where I want to be.

Just when I think I've figured out life, another "aha" moment surprises me, and another layer presents itself, like the veneer of stars in the sky, backed by another layer, and another—to what end? And if there is an end, what's on the other side of that? An endless story for the universe and the wealthy peasant.

If I should leave this planet without finishing my next book, *Grab Life by the Roots, and Bonsai the Shit Out of It,* I want get your attention as I used to with the girls when I told them I was taking them to the bathroom for a little chat, using my motherly tone of course, to tell you:

Your life is your responsibility, not someone else's. If we hang on to what has happened in our lives, blame others, or live for the approval of others, we put our souls on hold. We are individual expressions of humanity, and we will never learn to appreciate and celebrate our differences until we learn to appreciate and love ourselves. My favourite quote of all time is:

Don't ask what the world needs.
Ask what makes you come alive and go do it.
Because what the world needs is people who have come alive.

—Howard Thurman

Live from your soul, not your head. Listen to your longings; They are signals from your true self, niggling you to get back in your own boat. When you go with your own flow, the ripple effect will impact the world around you. When there are enough people coming alive, that is when the tides will turn, and the world will become a better place.

www.ingramcontent.com/pod-product-compliance
Lightning Source LLC
Chambersburg PA
CBHW051903090426
42811CB00003B/446